FRUTTI

JOHN BYRNE

TUTTI FRUTTI

JOHN BYRNE

CAST	*in alphabetical order*
Dennis	Kenneth Bryans
Vincent	Tam Dean Burn
Fud	Barrie Hunter
Noreen	Pauline Knowles
Glenna	Helen Mallon
Bomba	John McGlynn
Stuart	Alan McHugh
Lachie	Gavin Mitchell
Janice Toner	Julie Wilson Nimmo
Eddie Clockerty	John Ramage
Suzy Kettles	Dawn Steele
Danny McGlone	Tom Urie
Sheena Fisher	Clare Waugh

TOUR DATES

HIS MAJESTY'S THEATRE, ABERDEEN
FRI 22–SAT 30 SEPT (NOT SUNDAY) 7.30PM
MATINEES – SAT 23 & SAT 30 SEPT 2.30PM

KING'S THEATRE, EDINBURGH
TUE 3–SAT 7 OCT 7.30PM
MATINEES – WED 4 & SAT 7 OCT 2.30PM

A co-production with
His Majesty's Theatre,
Aberdeen

Tony Cownie	Director
Neil McArthur	Musical Director
Neil Murray	Designer
Jeanine Davies	Lighting Designer
Matt McKenzie	Sound Designer
John Alder	Video Designer

Gemma Swallow	Production Manager
Martin Woolley	Technical Manager
Aileen Sherry	Costume Supervisor
Mhairi Burton	Lighting Technician
Stephen Jones	Sound Technician
Ed Clarke	Production Sound Engineer
Ruth Crighton	Company Stage Manager
Sunita Hinduja	Deputy Stage Manager
Alison Brodie	Assistant Stage Manager
Tracey Farrell	Assistant Stage Manager
Stephanie Thorburn	Wardrobe Assistant

TUTTI FRUTTI
was first performed at
HIS MAJESTY'S THEATRE, ABERDEEN
on Friday 22 September 2006

THE COMPANY

JOHN BYRNE (Writer)

Born in Paisley in 1940, John Byrne is a writer and artist of international stature. He has been described by New Statesman as the first post-modernist from Paisley. John wrote the popular, BAFTA award-winning *Tutti Frutti* for BBC Television in 1987.

John is a distinguished playwright, best known for *The Slab Boys Trilogy*. His other plays include an adaptation of *Uncle Varick* for the Royal Lyceum, *Writers' Cramp, Normal Service, Cara Coco* and *Colquhoun and Macbryde*. He has also designed for the Traverse, 7:84, Hampstead Theatre, Bush Theatre and Scottish Opera.

John followed Tutti Frutti with *Your Cheatin' Heart* in 1990, again for the BBC.

As an artist, John's first London one man show was held at the Portal Gallery in 1967, while he was working as a carpet designer with A.F Stoddart in Elderslie. His work is held in major collections in Scotland and abroad.

JOHN ALDER (Video Designer)

John is an award-winning composer and film maker/ editor who has worked extensively in various areas of media and the arts. Starting out as a founder member of The Jags, he has progressed onto working as a session guitarist and vocalist with producers such as Steve Levine and Simon Humphrey, playing with acts such as The Beach Boys, Ziggy Marley and the Melody Makers and P. P. Arnold, as well as releasing the single *Believin' It All*, co-written by Boy George and produced by Steve Levine.

John moved on to writing music for television and has produced many tunes for BBC1, BBC2, Channel 4 and Sky TV. Work with theatre companies includes Northern Stage, Quarantine, Walk the Plank and Théâtre du Styx.

As well as touring nationally, his video and music have been played in France, Holland and Finland as well as at the Newcastle AVFest.

KENNETH BRYANS (Dennis)

Theatre work includes: *Tartuffe, Julius Caesar, Taming of the Shrew, Travesties, Merlin, A Family Affair* and *Juno and the Paycock* (Royal Lyceum), *Good Things* (Scottish Tour), *Justifying War* (Tricycle Theatre), *Henry IV Parts I & II, Henry V* (RSC), *The Colour of Justice* (Royal National Theatre and Tour), *The Cosmonaut's, Last Message to the Woman he Once Loved in the Soviet Union* (Paines Plough), *You'll Have Had Your Hole* (Astoria, London), *All My Sons* (Bristol Old Vic), *Wolf Kisses* (Royal Court), *Passing Places, Sharp Shorts, The Collection, The Bench, Hardie & Baird - The*

Last Days (Traverse), *Unidentified Human Remains* and *The True Nature of Love* (Hampstead), *A Man With Connections* (Perth Rep & Tour), *Aladdin* (Stirling), *Comedy of Errors* (Perth Rep), *Glengarry Glen Ross* (Tron Theatre).

Television work includes: *Taggart* (SMG), *The Bill* (Thames), *Millport, People Like Us, Looking After Jo Jo, A Mug's Game, Takin' Over the Asylum, Down Among the Big Boys, Gas and Candles, City Lights* and *The Justice Game* (BBC), *Deacon Brodie* (Tiger Aspect/BBC), *Barty and the Moonmen* (Baldycoots/ BBC), *Rockface* (Union Pictures), *Blue Murder* (Carlton), *Medical Ethics* (Scotland), *Wycliffe* (HTV), *Dr Finlay* (STV), *Finney* (Zenith).

Film work includes: *PU-239* (HBO Castell Films), *Mojo* (Mojo Films), *An Urban Ghost Story* (Living Spirit Pictures), *Macbeth* (Cromwell Films), *Shallow Grave* (Figment Films), *The Near Room* (Near Room Productions).

Radio work includes: *Kindling, Antoinette & Dougee, Word of Mouth, With Great Pleasure* and *My Mammy and Me* (BBC Radio).

TAM DEAN BURN (Vincent)

Theatre work includes: *Home Edinburgh* (National Theatre of Scotland), *Mary Stuart* (Donmar Warehouse and Apollo West End), *The Cutting Room, Venice Preserved, The Cherry Orchard, Observe the Sons of Ulster Marching Towards the Somme, Scrooge, Peer Gynt, The Pleasure Man* (Glasgow Citizens'), *Filth* (Citizens', National Tour and Calgary, Canada), *Platonov* (Almeida), *Berkoff's Messiah* (Edinburgh Assembly), *Headstate* (Lemon Tree and tour).

Television work includes: *River City, Taggart* (STV), *Helen West* (ITV), *Longford* (Channel 4).

Radio work includes: Ongoing solo show on resonancefm.com including *The Complete Poems of William Blake*. Tam has also directed and performed in many live radio plays for resonancefm.com.

Directing credits include: *William Burroughs Caught in Possession of the Rime of the Ancient Mariner* (Citizens' Theatre), *Sniperculture* (Traverse) and *Cruel Brittania* (London Scala) all written by Johnny Brown for Underground Utopia.

Audiobook work includes: *Trainspottng, Filth, Glue, Porno* (Irvine Welsh), *The Cutting Room* (Louise Welsh, RNIB).

Tam would like to thank his guitar teacher, Mick Slaven.

TONY COWNIE (Director)

Directing credits include: *Two* (RPM Arts Ltd & Michael Harrison), *Laurel and Hardy, A Life in the Theatre, The Taming of the Shrew, The Playboy of the Western World, Sleeping Beauty, The Princess and the Goblin, Miseryguts,*

Beauty and the Beast, The Comedy of Errors, Britannia Rules, Three Sisters, The Hypochondriak and *Cinderella* (Royal Lyceum), *Backpacker Blues* (Oran Mor), *The Woman Who Cooked Her Husband* (Tour), *The Laird O' Grippy* (Dundee Rep), the Herald Angel-winning *Empty Jesters* (Traverse), *Shanghaied* (Nippy Sweeties), *The King of Scotland* (Talking Dogs) and *Tartuffe* (QMC). Tony was also director of the UK Holocaust Memorial ceremony at the Usher Hall.

JEANINE DAVIES (Lighting Designer)

Jeanine's theatre work includes: *Home East Lothian* (National Theatre of Scotland*), Sweet Bird of Youth, Talented Mr. Ripley, Gypsy, Macbeth, Measure For Measure* (Dundee Rep), *Les Liaisons, Tartuffe, Laurel And Hardy (& Dublin Festival), All My Sons, Monks, Look Back In Anger (& Bath), A Madman Sings to the Moon, Uncle Varik, A View From The Bridge (& No 1 tour)* and *Misery Guts* (Royal Lyceum), *Pitlochry Season 2005, Lareigne* and *Uncanny* (X Factor Dance Company), *Almost But Not Quite* (Dancebase) and *Lifeboat* (both Edinburgh Festival 2005), *The Woman Who Cooked Her Husband (tour), Zlata's Diary, Werewolves* (Communicado*), Don Pasquale* (Scottish Opera Go Round), *Ay Carmela* (Traverse), *The BFG* (West End), *Cat On A Hot Tin Roof,* (Nottingham, Coventry, Royal Lyceum), *To Reach the Clouds, Angels Amongst The Trees, Polygraph,* (Nottingham Playhouse), Clockwork (ROH Linbury Studio), *A Christmas Carol* (Derby), *The Broken Heart* (RSC), *Il Re Pastore* (Classical Opera),*Tom's Midnight Garden* (Unicorn/New York).

BARRIE HUNTER (Fud)

Theatre work includes: *No Mean City, Swing Hammer Swing, Wizard of Oz, Pinocchio* (Citizens' Theatre), *Spending Frank, Trumpets & Raspberries* (Borderline), *Gypsy, Macbeth* (Dundee Rep), *Hot Air* (Oran Mor), *Breathing House, Victory, Misery Guts, Comedy of Errors, Woyzeck, Guys & Dolls, A View From The Bridge* (Royal Lyceum), *The Odd Couple, Into the Woods, Worzel Gummidge, Whistle Down the Wind* (Byre Theatre), *Sweeney Todd, Macbeth* (Courtyard), *3 Steps to Heaven* (1st Base), *Die Fledermaus* (Scottish Opera), *Mother Goose, Sleeping Beauty, Aladdin, Babes In The Wood* (King's Theatre*), The Big Picnic* (The Shed), *Our Bad Magnet* (Tron Theatre).

Television work includes: *Still Game, Velvet Soup 1 & 2, Stacey Stone, Change and Liberty, Jess the Border Collie, Life of Jolly, The Big Picnic* (BBC).

PAULINE KNOWLES
(Noreen)

Theatre work includes: *Gorgeous Avatar, The Trestle in Pope Lick Creek, Heritage, Knives in Hens* (Traverse), *Solemn Mass for a Full Moon in Summer* (Traverse/ Barbican), *Macbeth. A Doll's House, King Lear, Peter Pan* (Theatre Babel), *A Scot's Quair* (TAG), *Vassa* (Almeida), *Shining Souls* (Old Vic*), The Speculator* (Edinburgh International Festival), *Swing Hammer Swing* (Citizens'), *Cuttin' A Rug* (Royal Lyceum), *Misery* (Rapture Theatre Company), *Martha* (Catherine Wheels), *Twelfth Night* (Salisbury Playhouse).

Television work includes: *Man Hunter* (BBC), *Taggart* (STV).

Radio work includes: *Subutu Passage* (BBC).

HELEN MALLON
(Glenna)

This is Helen's professional debut since graduating from RSAMD in July, 2006.

Theatre work includes: *Sky High and After That* (Citizens' Theatre/RSAMD), *Last Supper, Comedy of Errors, Three Sisters* and *Diaspora* (Tron Theatre/National Theatre of Scotland/RSAMD), *Two (*Zero Six Productions), *Beowulf* (The Arches), *Kings of the Midden, Blethertoun Braes* (Itchy Coo).

Film work includes: *Senseless* (Plum Films/Matador).

NEIL McARTHUR
(Musical Director)

Theatre credits as Composer/Arranger/Musical Director include: *Ma Rainey's Black Bottom, A Streetcar Named Desire, The Villains' Opera, Oh! What a Lovely War, Snakehips, Fix-Up, Elmina's Kitchen, His Girl Friday* (Royal National Theatre), *Tamar's Revenge* (RSC), *Sex, Chips and Rock 'N' Roll (*Manchester Royal Exchange), *Half a Sixpence, The Wizard of Oz, Bad Girls - The Musical* (West Yorkshire Playhouse), *Cat on a Hot Tin Roof* (West End/Broadway), *Five Guys Named Moe* (West End/Broadway/Australia/US Tour), *Harry Nilsson's The Point* (Mermaid), *Blues in the Night* (West End), *High Society* (Sheffield Crucible), *Great Balls of Fire: The Jerry Lee Lewis Story* (Birmingham Rep/West End), *Maria Friedman by Special Arrangement* (West End), *Joseph Fiennes' Shakespeare* (Tibet), *Up on the Roof, Holes in the Skin* (Chichester).

TV credits include: *Frank Stubbs* (ITV), *Eastenders, Chalk, Elmina's Kitchen* and *The Paul Merton Series* (BBC), *The Ancient Mariner, Dressing for Breakfast* (Channel 4) and *Blues in the Night* (Thames TV).

Film credits include: *Victory, The Boat People* (Skyline Films).

Neil was also a member of Harvey and the Wallbangers (1982-1987).

JOHN McGLYNN (Bomba)

Theatre work includes: *Dracula* and *Snow Queen* (Royal Lyceum), *Songs for Stray Cats* (Paines Plough), *Macbeth, Thérèse Raquin* and *Cherry Orchard* (Nottingham Playhouse).

Television work includes: *Casualty* (BBC), *Doctors* (BBC), *River City* (BBC), *Dr Finlay Casebook* (BBC), *Heartbeat* (Yorkshire TV), *Rosemary and Thyme* (Carnival Films), *The Court Room* (Mersey Television), *The Inspector Lynley Mysteries - A Traitor to Memory* (BBC), *The Planman* (Ideal World), *Taggart* (Scottish Television), *The Swap* (Greenlit Productions), *Coronation Street* (Granada Television), *Hero of the Hour* (LWT), *The Last Musketeer* (STV), *Psychos* (Kudos), *Trust* (Red Rooster Productions), *Ruth Rendell - The Orchard Walls* (Blue Heaven), *Silent Witness* and *Nervous Energy* (BBC).

Film work includes: *The Queen* (Granada Screen (2005) Ltd), *Wimbledon* (Love All Films), *Gangs of New York* (Paradise Square), *The Emperor's New Clothes* (Bonaparte Films), *Les Miserables* (Mandalay).

Radio work Includes: *The Duel* and *Dr Finlay - Adventures Of A Black Bag* (BBC), *Beware of the Trains* (Fiction Factory).

ALAN McHUGH (Stuart)

Theatre work includes: *Accidental Death of an Anarchist* (Borderline), *Tally's Blood* (Byre Theatre), *Sunset Song* (Prime Productions), *A Passionate Woman* (Perth Rep), *Three Steps To Heaven* (1st Base), *The Jolly Beggars, Bedfellows* and *The Silver Darlings* (Wildcat Productions), *The Grapes of Wrath* (7:84/Dundee Rep), *A Taste of Honey* (The Arches), *Jack and the Beanstalk* (Qdos), *Aladdin* (Adam Smith Theatre).

Television work includes: *Dear Green Place* (EffinGee Productions), *Jess the Border Collie* (IWC Media), *High Road* (STV), *Battlefield Britain Culloden* (BBC 2), *Sea of Souls, River City, Rab C Nesbitt* (BBC Scotland).

Film work includes: *Small Moments* (Oxygen Films) and *Wild County* (Gabriel Films).

MATT McKENZIE (Sound Designer)

Matt has designed the sound for venues including the Lyric Theatre Hammersmith, Yvonne Arnaud Theatre, Guildford, Chichester Festival Theatre, Derby Playhouse, Haymarket Theatre, Leicester, Traverse, Edinburgh, the Bush Theatre, The Donmar Warehouse, Soho Theatre and theatres in London's West End.

He was Sound Supervisor for the Peter Hall Seasons at The Old Vic and The Piccadilly. Work for the RSC includes *Family Reunion, Henry V, The Duchess of Mafli, Hamlet, The Lieutenant of Inishmore, Julius Caesar* and *A Midsummer Night's Dream.*

Matt's musical work includes: *The Bells are Ringing* and *Talk of the Steamie* (Greenwich), *Love off the Shelf* (Nuffield Theatre), *Oh What A Lovely War!, Company, Christmas Carol, Sweeney Todd* and *Into The Woods* (Derby Playhouse), *Forbidden Broadway, Blues in the Night* and *Tango Argentino* (West End), *Car Man* (West End and International Tour), *Putting It Together* and *The Gondoliers, How to Succeed in Business Without Really Trying* and *Carousel* (Chichester Festival Theatre) and the co-sound design of *Tess* (Savoy Theatre) and *Alice in Wonderland* (RSC).

He is also Associate Sound Designer for the 2006 Chichester Festival.

GAVIN MITCHELL (Lachie)

Theatre work includes: *Casanova* (Suspect Culture), *Travels With My Aunt, The Housekeeper, Macbeth, Edward II, Mother Courage* (Citizens' Theatre), *Still Life, Conquest of the South Pole, One Flew Over the Cuckoo's Nest* (Raindog), *Dead Funny* (Borderline), *Thebans, Greeks, Peter Pan* and *Don Juan* (Theatre Babel), *Habitats* (Tron Theatre/EK Prod).

Television work includes: *Still Game, Monarch of the Glen, Velvet Soup, Revolver, Days That Shock The World, Donovan Quick, Mr Wymi, Cardiac Arrest, Takin' Over The Asylum* (BBC), *Taggart* (STV).

Film work includes: *Breaking The Waves, The Three Musketeers* (Zentropa), *Mandancing* (IA Productions), *Cry for Bobo* (Forged Films), *Being Human* (Enigma Films).

NEIL MURRAY (Designer)

Neil Murray is Associate Director and Designer at Northern Stage. Since 1992 his directing/designing credits with the company include: *Great Expectations, Kaput Cinzano/Smirnova's Birthday, Pandora's Box* (with Emma Rice), *The Tiger's Bride, The Three Penny Opera, Carmen, They Shoot Horses Don't They?, Thérèse Raquin, The Swan* and numerous Christmas shows, including *Beauty and the Beast, The Snow Queen* and *Grimm Tales*. His latest piece for Northern Stage is *The Little Prince*.

He has also designed most of the company's other work, including *Wings of Desire, Blood Wedding, The Ballroom of Romance, A Clockwork Orange, Animal Farm, 1984, The Black Eyed Roses, Romeo and Juliet, Twelfth Night, Edmund, Not I, The Dumb Waiter* and *Homage to Catalonia* (co-production with West Yorkshire Playhouse, Teatre Romea, Barcelona and MC Bobigny'93, Paris).

Previously, he was Associate Director/Designer at Dundee Rep for 10 years and prior to that he was Resident Artist in Theatre at the Arts Lab in Birmingham where he created mixed-media theatre pieces which toured internationally.

He continues to work with other companies when time

allows. Recent work includes: *1001 Nights Now* and *Wings of Desire* (Betty Nansen Theatre, Copenhagen), *Princess and the Goblin*, *Laurel and Hardy* and *Mrs Warren's Profession* (Royal Lyceum), *Like Water for Chocolate* (Teatre San Frontiers).

JULIE WILSON NIMMO
(Janice Toner)

Theatre work includes: *Shining Souls* (Tron Theatre), *The Magic Island* (TAG), *Beauty and the Beast* (Citizens'), *Balamory Live* (National Tour).

Television work includes: *Balamory* (BBC Scotland), *Chewin' The Fat* (Comedy Unit), *Stand and Deliver* (Paralax Pictures), *Rab C Nesbitt, Baldy Man, Involuntary* (Comedy Unit), *Young Persons Guide to Becoming a Rock Star* (Channel 4), *Murder Rooms, Three Years in a Toilet, Claire In The Community* and *Pulp Video* (BBC).

Film work includes: *Mrs Caulticots Cabbage War* (Mersey Films), *My Life So Far* (Enigma Films), *The Slab Boys* (Skreba – Films), *The Wrong Blonde* (Pathe), *Afterlife* (Gabriel Films), *Magdalene Sisters* (PSP Films).

JOHN RAMAGE
(Eddie Clockerty)

Theatre work includes: *Elizabeth Gordon Quinn* (National Theatre of Scotland), *Mince, Measure for Measure, Cabaret, A Winter's Tale, Land O'Cakes, A Midsummer Night's Dream, Playboy Of The Western World, The Seagull, The Princess and the Goblin* and *The Night Before Christmas* (Dundee Rep Ensemble), *The Importance of Being Earnest, Funny Money, A Little Hotel on the Side* (Pitlochry Festival Theatre), *HMS Pinafore, The Mikado, Peter Pan, Rough Crossing, The Boyfriend, A Christmas Carol* and five pantomimes as Dame/Co-writer (Perth Theatre), *Your Turn to Clean the Stairs, Shining Souls, Widows* (Traverse), *Salvation, Cinderella, Jack And The Beanstalk* (Tron Theatre).

Film and television work includes: *The High Life, Rab C. Nesbitt* (BBC).

Radio work includes: many radio dramas, regular presenter of *Hopscotch* for BBC Education, writer/actor for two series of *The Daily Sketch*.

Directing credits include: *Kabaret* (Stellar Quines), *The Last of the Lairds* (Perth Theatre), more than 20 productions for Queen Margaret University College School of Drama.

DAWN STEELE
Suzi Kettles

Theatre work includes: *Rainbow Kiss (Royal Court Theatre), The Slab Boys Trilogy* (Traverse), *Electra* and *Medea* (Theatre Babel).

Television work includes: *Sea of Souls* (BBC Scotland), *The Key* (BBC), *Monarch of the Glen* and *Snoddy* (BBC Scotland), *Tinsel Town* (Raindog/BBC), *Highlander, War and Peace* (Gaumont TV), *Haywire* (BBC), *Split Second* (BBC).

Film work includes: *Tabloid TV* (David Blair), *Club Le Monde* (Club Le Monde Prods), *Gregory's 2 Girls* (Younglak).

Radio work includes: *Crossing the Line* (BBC).

TOM URIE
(Danny McGlone)

Theatre work includes: *Cinderella* (First Family Entertainment), *Singalong-A-Sound-Of-Music* (Singalong Productions), *Loot* and *The Jungle Book* (Byre Theatre), *The Steamie* (Double Edge).

Television work includes: *Almost Angelic, The Karen Dunbar Show, Only and Excuse, Head to Head With Britney Spears* and *Chewin' The Fat* (Comedy Unit), *Yo! Diary* (Comedy Unit/CBBC), *Ancient Greeks* (BBC), *Saint Anthony's Day Off.*

Film work includes: *Psychotica* (Ink) and *Rogue Farm* (SMG).

Radio work includes: *Watson's Wind Up, Coming Home, Karen Dunbar Show, Ronan the Amphibian* (Comedy Unit), *Let's Write a Story* (BBC Scotland/Radio 4).

CLARE WAUGH
(Sheena Fisher)

Theatre work includes: *Oz King of Clubs* (Ozmosis Productions), *Head On* (Boilerhouse Theatre Company), *Little Snow White* and *The Little Mermaid* (Cumbernauld Theatre Company), *Blackout* (Vanishing Point), *For What We Are About To Receive* (Brunton Theatre Company), *Sound Pictures* (The Arches), *Beauty And The Beast* (Royal Lyceum), *Last Night* (Fablevision), *Sleeping Beauty, Cinderella* and *Jack and the Beanstalk* (Tell Tale/ Wish Productions/Kilmarnock), *Gail's Shoes* (Acting Up), *Soor Plooms* and *Jawbreakers* (Court Of Miracles), *Burns On The Solway* and *Ida Tamson* (Oran Mor).

Television work includes: *The Last Laugh* (BBC 3), *Taggart* (STV), *Floor Show* (BBC Scotland), *Revolver* (BBC), *Velvet Soup 2* (BBC Scotland), *Famous People,* (Walk/Clemments), *Focus* (BBC).

Radio work includes: *Nice Device* (BBC Scotland).

Directing credits includes: *Millenium* and *Media* (Dramart Productions).

NATIONAL
THEATRE
OF SCOTLAND

Scottish theatre has always been for the people, led by great performances, great stories or great playwrights. The National Theatre of Scotland exists to build a new generation of theatre-goers as well as reinvigorating the existing ones; to create theatre on a national and international scale that is contemporary, confident and forward-looking; to bring together brilliant artists, composers, choreographers and playwrights; and to exceed expectations of what and where theatre can be.

The National Theatre of Scotland has no building. Instead, we are taking theatre all over Scotland, working with the existing venues, touring and creating work within the theatre community. We have no bricks-and mortar institutionalism to counter, nor the security of a permanent home in which to develop. All our money and energy can be spent on creating the work. Our theatre will take place in the great buildings – Edinburgh's Royal Lyceum and Glasgow's Citizens' Theatre – but also in site specific locations, community halls and drill halls, car parks and forests.

Since our launch in February 2006 we have produced:

- *HOME* - an extraordinary opening event which took place in ten locations across the country
- *FALLING* – a promenading site-specific performance co-produced with Poorboy
- *THE WOLVES IN THE WALLS* – a musical pandemonium for all the family co-produced with Improbable
- *ROAM* – a site-specific event at Edinburgh Airport co-produced with Grid Iron
- *THE CRUCIBLE* – a touring professional and community cast event co-produced with TAG

- *ELIZABETH GORDON QUINN* – a major revival of Chris Hannan's Scottish classic
- *BLACK WATCH* – an unauthorized biography of the legendary Scottish regiment
- *REALISM* – a world premiere of Anthony Neilson's new work co-produced with the Edinburgh International Festival
- *ENSEMBLE* – a company of seven performers touring towns and villages across the country with a repertory of three plays: *JULIE* adapted by Zinnie Harris from the Strindberg play; *MANCUB* by Douglas Maxwell; and *GOBBO* devised and created by David Greig and Wils Wilson.

During these inaugural six months we have won a clutch of awards. At the Critics' Awards for Theatre in Scotland, we won Best Ensemble, Best Technical Presentation and Best Theatre Production for *ROAM,* Best Children's Show and Best Design for *HOME: East Lothian* and Best Music for *HOME: Shetland.* In August we became the first company to appear at both the Edinburgh International and Fringe Festivals, receiving a Herald Angel for *REALISM* and a Herald Angel, a Fringe First, a List Best Theatre Writing Award and a Stage Award for Best Ensemble for *BLACK WATCH.*

This autumn, along with *TUTTI FRUTTI,* we are also touring a new version of Schiller's *MARY STUART* by David Harrower in a co-production with the Citizens' and the Royal Lyceum, and *PROJECT MACBETH,* an NTS Learn production.

For more information about
the National Theatre of Scotland, visit
www.nationaltheatrescotland.com
or call +44 (0) 141 221 0970

FOR THE NATIONAL THEATRE OF SCOTLAND

The Board of Directors

Richard Findlay (Chair), Anne Bonnar, Allan Burns, Peter Cabrelli, Maggie Kinloch, Iain More, Donald Smith, Irene Tweedie

The Company

Karen Allan	Learn Project Manager
Lynn Atkinson	Accounts Assistant
Davey Anderson	Director in Residence
Kim Beveridge	Digital Artist
Niall Black	Production Manager
Sheryl Brosnan	PA to the Directors
Neil Campbell	Young Company Actor
Kate Cattell	Project Administrator
Colin Clark	Web Editor
Steve Collins	Young Company Director
Grahame Coyle	Ensemble Production Manager
Cameron Duncan	Communications Consultant
Vicky Featherstone	Artistic Director and Chief Executive
Gillian Gourlay	Learning & Outreach Manager
Sarah Gray	Young Company Producer
Maryam Hamidi	Young Company Actor
Fiona Hanrahan	Office Administrator
Pamela Hay	Young Company Producer
Chris Hay	Deputy Production Manager
Lois Hay	Finance Manager
Anne Henderson	Casting Director
Scott Hoatson	Young Company Actor
Marianne McAtarsney	Marketing Manager
Kirstin McLean	Young Company Actor
Ken Mill	Finance Director
Neil Murray	Executive Director
Caroline Newall	Workshop Director
Susan O'Neill	Communications Officer (Temporary)
Toni O'Neill	Project Co-Ordinator
Jessica Richards	Company Manager
Emma Schad	Press Manager
Simon Sharkey	Associate Director - New Learning
Allan Smillie	Finance Assistant
Gemma Swallow	Tutti Frutti Production Manager
John Tiffany	Associate Director - New Work
Ben Walmsley	Administration & Operations Manager

John Byrne
Tutti Frutti

with illustrations by the author

faber and faber

First published in 2006
by Faber and Faber Limited
3 Queen Square, London WC1N 3AU

Typeset by Country Setting, Kingsdown, Kent CT14 8ES
Printed in England by Bookmarque, Croydon, Surrey

A CIP record for this book
is available from the British Library

ISBN 978-0-571-23613-8
ISBN 0-571-23613-8

2 4 6 8 10 9 7 5 3 1

Characters

Danny
Suzi
Vincent
Bomba
Fud
Dennis
Eddie
Miss Toner
Glenna
Noreen
Sheena Fisher
TV Director
Nurse
Lachie
Caller / Young Blonde Woman
Stuart
Abernethy
Shooby-Doo Dolls
Priest
Mourners
Dentist's Patients

Big Jazza

Act One

From the darkness comes the voice of the Priest.

Priest Out of the depths I have cried to Thee, O Lord. Lord, hear my voice. Let Thine ears be attentive to the voice of my supplication . . . if Thou, O Lord, would grant it . . .

Lights slowly up on Big Jazza McGlone's funeral service. The mourners – Eddie Clockerty and Miss Toner, the widow Big Theresa, her daughters Doreen and Brenda Lee, Dennis Sproul (the Majestics' roadie), with Big Jazza's primrose-yellow stage suit folded in his arms, and sundry others gathered round the grave.

Priest Lord, hear us.

Mourners Lord, graciously hear us.

Bomba, Fud *and* **Vincent** (*offstage, sing*)
'There are just three steps to Heaven . . .
One, two, three . . .
Look, and you will plainly see . . .' (*Etc.*)

The three surviving members of the band appear, bearing a huge floral tribute in the shape of a Fender Strat. They move with great dignity to the graveside and, still essaying the Eddie Cochran classic 'a capella', lay the monster wreath reverently on the ground, before stepping back and adjusting their Ray-Bans. They are attired identically in black. The song carries through to its conclusion as the Priest silently intones the Latin burial service, sprinkles holy water into lair.

Priest And, lo, there came the voice of an Angel . . .

Offstage screech of brakes, clunk of taxi door slamming shut.

Danny (*offstage*) What d'you mean, you canny take American dollars? You should've told us that at the bloody airport!

Eddie gives Dennis a nod. Dennis sets off irritably to settle the latecomer's taxi fare.

(*Offstage.*) I'm not shoutin', I'm here to pay ma respects at ma brother's funeral!

Bomba, Fud and Vincent exchange quizzical looks. All turn to look at Eddie. Eddie remains his enigmatic self as he slips the Priest a bung.

Sound of taxicab drawing away – tootle on horn.

(*Offstage.*) Aye, and you, ya deadbeat!

Danny appears, in a gaberdine suit creased to buggery, a plastic bag bearing the iconic I LOVE NY *logo in his mitt. Dennis, at his heels, is tucking an empty wallet back into his hip pocket.*

Dennis (*to Eddie*) That's fourteen quid you owe us.

Eddie (*ignoring him*) Danny Boy . . .

He approaches Danny, hand outstretched. Danny looks blank.

Eddie. Eddie Clockerty. So good of you to come all this way at such short notice. Don't you think, Miss Toner?

He looks meaningfully at Danny, who is donning dark glasses from the plastic bag. Miss Toner looks blank. Eddie looks meaningfully at the grave, then at Danny. Miss Toner just stares.

Danny So what was it . . . a heart attack, yeah?

Bring up Radio DJ.

Danny

Radio DJ . . . And the tributes are still pouring in for James McGlone, better known to Scottish music fans as Big Jazza, the charismatic frontman for the Majestics, who said 'Goodbye, Cruel World' in classic rock'n'roll style in the wee small hours of Tuesday morning when the vehicle he was driving careered headlong into a bus shelter on the South Side of the city whilst making his way back to the band's HQ with a carry-out order of kebabs for himself and fellow Majestics, Bomba, Fud and Vinnie. Here's the one that took them to Number Seven in the charts in 1962 . . . Rest in peace, Your Heavyweight Majesty . . .

Dennis lets stage outfit drop into the grave. Big Jazza and the Majestics on screen: 'No Particular Place to Go'.

Lights up on Danny and Dennis, Danny perplexed.

Danny Where ur we? Thought we wur goin' back to Big Theresa's?

Dennis Naw . . . *they're* goin' back to Big Theresa's – O'Donnell, MacAteer an' Diver . . . bass, percussion an' lead guitar. Plus yours truly, Dennis Sproul, transport an' what-huv-you.

Danny Sufferin' God, he was *ma* brother . . . I can surely go back to his place furra drink after his funeral!

Dennis Listen, Danny Boy, thur's three outfits where blood ties don't count fur that much . . . (*Snaps fingers.*) The Mafia – the Magic Circle – an' the Majestics. (*Makes to go, stops.*) An' before you say anythin', don't imagine yur the only one that's peeved . . . I've been thur roadie fur as long as I can remember an' if it hudny been fur that stupit brother of yours huvvin a cravin' fur *kebabs* the other night I was onty four per cent of the gross from this twenty-five-gig Silver Jubilee tour that Eddie Clockerty's had me settin' up fur the past twelve months, exceptin' it isny gonny happen now, so that's the other reason yur no' goin' back to Big Theresa's . . . What the hell've *you* got to cry inty yur beer about? Nothin', right! (*Turns on his heels.*) Like they say back in yur adopted city, 'Huv a nice day, Danny Boy!'

He exits. Danny is left standing alone, clutching his plastic bag. The dying refrain of the Majestics' one and only hit record, 'No Particular Place To Go', echoes and re-echoes in Danny's head as Dennis lets in the clutch of the Transit van and moves off.

Danny slowly lowers himself onto a chair as the lights come up in Chimmy Chunga's. Suzi Kettles makes her way past his table with a tray – does a double-take.

Suzi Danny?

Danny glances up.

Danny McGlone?

Danny lifts his shades as Suzi moves in for a closer look.

It's me . . . Suzi.

Danny 'Suzi'?

Suzi Suzi Kettles. C'mon, cut the kiddin' . . . Glasgow School of Art – you were in Third-Year Drawing and Painting. I used to chum you and your pal up the road from the subway – dirty lookin' individual with hair down to here and a banjo case full of empty beer bottles . . .

Danny That would be Abernethy . . . as in biscuit.

Suzi That's him. He was in here not that long ago in a blazer and tie, said you were working in New York . . .

something to do with the entertainment scene, he was saying. What you doing back here?

Danny I came across fur ma brother.

Suzi Aw, yeah, how's he doing? Is he still playing with that band . . . What was it they called themselves again?

Danny The Majestics. Naw, he's . . . er . . . jacked it in.

Suzi That seems a shame. Still, if you're not making much of a dent in the charts . . .

Danny As opposed to what . . . bus shelters, we talkin'?

Suzi I remember them playing that Art School hop when you were violently sick all down the back of Joyce Quigley's kaftan . . . You had me in stitches – you wore these really strange trousers . . . So what happened to them? I haven't seen them in yonks.

Danny Ma Old Dear gave them away to the ragman . . . She got a balloon fur them.

Suzi Your brother's band, quit actin' it.

Danny I seem to recall you wur a dog at Art School, Kettles.

Suzi Yeah, thanks . . . Like you were some kinda *hunk*? Right, what can I get you?

Danny It's comin' back to me now . . . sorta donkey-jacket effort wi' drainpipe jeans an' big tackitty boots. Boy Abernethy an' me used to draw lots to see who got *not* to sit next to you on the subway. I'll huv a big Martini – very dry.

Suzi The olives might be foosty . . . just to warn you.

Danny I'll live dangerously . . . plenty ice, yeah?

Suzi (*loudly*) One large Martini . . . plenty ice!

Danny Where's yur Gents? I huvny been since we flew over Newfoundland.

Suzi Through there – door with the tarantula stencilled on it. (*Watching him leave.*) God, Danny McGlone . . . what an ugly-lookin' big guy.

Lights up on Clockerty Enterprises office.

Miss Toner Pity about the Silver Jubilee tour, eh? Still, you canny very well send a band round the country fronted by a stiff, can you, Mr Clockerty?

Eddie No, Janice, but you can have the next best thing. Get me Wee Tommy Cairns on the telephone.

Miss Toner Don't be daft, Wee Tommy canny sing. Besides which, he's only this big – (*Places a hand at waist height. Picks up phone.*)

Eddie Stop acting the goat and get on with it. Did you not see me inclining my head towards Danny Boy, then at the grave, then back to Danny Boy?

Miss Toner (*dialling*) Aw, that? I thought that was jist some kinda Catholic boogie-woogie us Proddies wurny privy to . . . D'you want a coffee?

Eddie Did you not notice the remarkable similarity? It was positively breathtaking.

Miss Toner Between what an' what? A hole in the turf an' a guy in a gaberdine suit that looked like he'd jist fell out the baggage hold of a low-flyin' aircraft? Naw, canny say I did, Mr Clockerty.

Eddie Between the late Big Jazza and the newly arrived Danny Boy, ya stupid girl . . . (*Taking receiver from Miss Toner.*) Hullo, Tommy? Eddie Clockerty . . . Listen to this for a wheeze . . .

Blackout.

Lights up on art gallery.

Suzi You're a funny guy, McGlone.

Danny How? 'Cos I like foosty olives in ma big Martinis an' invite dolls furra stroll round ma favourite art gallery?

Suzi I would be upset if it was *my* only brother that'd just got himself killed in a car smash.

Danny C'mon, I hudny clapped eyes on the big palooka fur years, so I'm hardly gonny be doin' ma Greyfriars Bobby an' goin' out to lie on his grave. And I *am* upset . . . I mean, what's ma sister-in-law gonny do fur dosh now? The Carpet Discount Showroom in Shawlands'll huv to go, not to mention the ranch house in Cambuslang . . .

Suzi I don't believe it.

Danny Naw, straight up, it's even got a hitchin' rail at the front gate fur bikes an' saloon doors on the lavatory. Big Guy hud it built out the proceeds from thur hit single all them years ago.

Suzi I don't believe that all you can talk about is money at a time like this, McGlone.

Danny When better? Another coupla weeks an' the Sheriff's Officers'll be kickin' Big Theresa's door in. (*Running hand over modern sculpture.*) Amazin' what you can do wi' a big lumpa plasticine, innit?

Suzi What about your brother's motor car insurance?

Danny Accordin' to the police report, ma brother was six times over the legal limit, plus whatever it was he was shootin' up . . . an' it wasny his motor car, it was thur manager's.

Suzi Their manager's insurance, then.

Danny Wur talkin' Eddie Clockerty, sweetheart. Four baldy tyres an' a fake MOT. All he hus to say was his client took the motor without Clockerty Enterprises' say-so.

Suzi So he's a crook, this Clockerty person?

Danny Wouldny like to comment on that, Kettles, seein' as how it was him that paid fur ma air fare over.

Suzi So when're you going back to this – (*In cod Americanese.*) – 'terrific duplex apartment in the great thumpin' heart of the theatre district'?

Danny Oh, look . . . a Botticelli.

He makes to go off and look at the painting. Suzi grabs his arm.

Suzi Never heed the Botticelli, the boy Abernethy-as-in-biscuit was overheard bummin' to the bar staff about his 'big-time buddy' and how he had an open invite to 'go visit with you' any old time he fancied. C'mon, out with it, McGlone.

Danny Please, Suzi, wur in a public art gallery.

Suzi Cut it out, you know fine well what I'm getting at. Look at the state of you. If you really had a duplex in the middle of Manhattan you could afford to buy yourself a pair of socks.

She lifts Danny's trouser leg to reveal bare ankle.

Danny Okay, okay, it's a cruddy cold-water walk-up in the South Bronx. It *was* a duplex, but the only way to get to the upstairs bedroom was via the fire escape, an' we had a fire an' it got burnt an' fell off. Me an' this funny shoe salesman share the rent . . . While he's out poundin' the sidewalks lookin' fur customers wi' funny feet I'm in the fold-down cot catchin' up on ma shut-eye, then when he gets back I'm out poundin' the piana keys in this crummy joint in Jersey hopin' to get ma Green Card so I can go legit an' make some real dough . . . It's murder, I don't mind tellin' you. An' yur right about the suit . . . It was left folded up behind a radiator by a junkie that jumped off the roof of the buildin'. I got the janitor's boyfriend to take it in fur us. Huvny hud it off ma back in fourteen weeks. Aw, God, I've jist remembered thon guitar I got fur ma Christmas. Know what the bastart done?

Suzi Who's this, the janitor's boyfriend?

Danny Big Jazza . . . sawed the neck off an' used it furra cricket bat!

Suzi Here, blow your nose. (*Gives him tiny hanky.*)

Danny I've still got the strings somewhere.

Suzi What you need's a hot bath and a bite to eat, McGlone. C'mon, we'll go Dutch, there's a nice Greek place round the corner.

Danny Awright, as long as it isny . . .

Suzi Isny what?

Danny As long as it isny *kebabs*, right?

Lights up on Glenna's brand new flat. Shoes in hand, Fud and Bomba are still in mourning attire as they prowl around.

Bomba Two hooses, Fud. Even Elvis never had two hooses.

Fud This'll be hur, yeah? (*Picks up framed snapshot.*) I've got a twelve-year-old at home looks older'n this doll. What's got inty him, d'you suppose? Mind you, what one of us husny asked thurselves that question down the years, eh, Bomba?

Bomba Gimme that!

Snatches photo, slams it face down. Dennis appears with a tray of coffees.

Fud What d'*you* reckon to the *girlfriend*, Dennis?

Dennis I'm yur roadie, *ergo* . . . hear no evil, see no evil, speak no evil.

Bomba What d'you mean, '*ergo*'?

Dennis It's Latin fur 'that's yur coffees'.

Vincent appears. Dennis slips away in his motorcycle boots.

Bomba So, Vinnie . . . you wur sayin'?

Vincent (*dispensing coasters*) When?

Bomba At Big Theresa's . . . after the purvey.

Fud (*biting into coaster*) You no' got any Penguins, naw?

Vincent All I was sayin' was, supposin' we came up wi' somebody like . . . I don't know . . . a tad younger, mebbe?

Fud What about the man himself?

Bomba What you on about – what *man*?

Fud Tad Younger. Country blues howler from Banff. Used to sing wi' the Texas Scumbags 'fore they got religion an' turned inty the Rockabilly Bible Thumpers.

Bomba Drink yur coffee an' shut up, O'Donnell . . . (*To Vincent.*) About Springsteen's age, we talkin'?

Vincent Younger'n that even.

Fud Any younger'n Springsteen an' wur talkin' about an *apprentice*, Vinnie . . . (*To Bomba.*) Aye, okay, 'Shuttup an' drink yur coffee,' but I'm right an' you know it.

Bomba
B
1957

Dennis appears. Offstage cries of twins from Transit.

Dennis Huv you got thur sweeties?

Bomba Hang on . . . (*Starts searching through pockets.*) Carry on, Vincent. Bit younger'n Springsteen, you wur sayin'.

Vincent (*righting Glenna's photo, to Dennis*) Ho . . . yur *footwear*!

Bomba Never heed his bloody footwear . . . Younger'n Springsteen, yeah?

Dennis reluctantly removes motorcycle boots. Fud examines underside of new carpet. Vincent helps himself to whisky.

Fud You no' meant to huv some kinda underlay wi' this garbage, naw?

Bomba What wur you jist told, you? Wur doin' wur damndest to come up wi' a suitable candidate to replace a rock'n'roll legend so we can get the Majestics back on the road fur this Silver Jubilee malarkey an' consolidate twenty-five years of non-stop tourin', not huvvin' a leisurely stroll round a cut-price carpet warehouse wi' the wife an' weans on a Saturday afternoon, right!

Vincent Ho . . . less of the 'cut-price', pal, this 's a hunner-per-cent polypropylene wi' a reinforced nylon backin' at forty-four quid the square metre . . .

Offstage howls and an arhythmic Transit horn pumping as Bomba produces a poke of sweeties.

Bomba Forty-four quid, my arse . . . (*To Dennis.*) Here, give the wee fella two chocolate buttons an' a gold doubloon, the lassie can huv what's left in the sherbet fountain . . .

More howling offstage.

Och, I'll do it, you get yur bloody footwear back on . . . (*Loudly.*) Awright, can it, you pair . . . I'm comin'!

He leaves. Dennis scrambles into boots and totters after him.

Vincent Did you get a phone call last night?

Fud Who, me? Nup.

Vincent 'Cos I got one from Eddie.

Fud Aw, *that* phone call.

Vincent Aye, *that* phone call . . . So, what'd you think?

Fud I thought it was a bloody cheek phonin' at that time of night, the older kids an' I wur playin' poker – I hud a Jack flush.

Vincent About what Eddie was yappin' on about, ya clown. Aw that guff about 'resurrection' an' how if we play wur cards right wur aw gonny be 'saved'.

Fud He mebbe wants us to chuck in a coupla gospel numbers on the tour. See? I think Tad Younger's wur man right enough.

Vincent Shuttup an' drink yur coffee.

Bomba reappears. Vincent helps himself to another dollop of whisky.

Bomba Right, where wur we?

Vincent Jist askin' the boy there if he wants a top-up . . . You want a top-up, Francis?

Bomba (*controlling himself*) Where wur we *vis à vis* a replacement fur the band's lead vocal an' guitar strummer, the late Big Jazza McGlone, I'm askin'?

Vincent Well, the way I see it, we want somebody ballsy, right?

Vincent

Bomba looks to Fud. Fud looks sceptical.

Fud Mmm . . . No' too sure. I suppose if we got them a snug-fittin' hairpiece . . . (*Looking from Vincent to Bomba.*) What? S'that no' what he said? 'Somebody *baldy*', naw?

Bomba I'm not warnin' you again . . . Thur's too much at stake here fur comical detours, right? (*To Vincent.*) 'Ballsy's' good, yeah?

Fud 'Ballsy's' excellent – what else you got?

Vincent Somebody wi' bags of *charisma*, yeah?

Fud Absolutely vital . . . bitta 'charisma' goes a long way in ma book. No' too keen on bags of the stuff . . . Big Guy hud bags of charisma, look where that landed us.

Bomba Hate to say it, but the boy's right. We don't want *another* mad bastart.

Vincent (*plucking photo from TV set*) Naw, naw, I'm talkin' about somebody wi' *allure* . . .

Fud (*to Bomba*) Somebody wi' a what?

Vincent . . . Somebody *vibrant* . . . somebody *cool* an' at the same time sorta . . . *smoulderin'*, you with me?

Fud Aw aw.

Bomba With you? Wur way ahead of you, Diver . . . C'mon, O'Donnell, get yur footwear back on, wur leavin'.

Fud and Bomba head off.

Vincent Ho, come back here, ya clowns . . .

Bomba (*loudly*) Start the wagon, Dennis!

They disappear off, pursued by Vincent.

Vincent Yur makin' a big mistake, d'you hear? This chick's gonny be bigger n' Jonis Japlin . . .

A roar as the Transit van takes off along the street. Vincent disappears off.

(*Offstage.*) Janis Joplin . . . you jist wait! (*He reappears.*) Imbeciles! Eejits! *Morons!*

Lights up on Eddie on telephone.

Eddie What d'you mean, you left him outside the cemetery gates? You were under strict instructions not to let him out of your sight until . . . What d'you mean, 'Vincent's not going to be too happy with this arrangement'? *Bugger* Vincent, I've already run it past Wee Tommy and he thinks . . .

Miss Toner 'Scuse me, Mr Clockerty . . .

Eddie Not now, Janice . . . And he thinks . . . What d'you mean, *if* you find him? You bloody well better find him or . . . No, no, don't tell him that! Just say it's a benefit gig for his sister-in-law prior to the Silver Jubilee tour . . .

Miss Toner 'Scuse me, Mr Clockerty, but the boy McGlone –

Eddie No, on second thoughts, don't mention the Silver Jubilee tour, we'll cross that bridge when we come to it.

Miss Toner (*overlapping*) – the boy McGlone reversed the charges from a payphone at some Greek dive while you wur in the Gents –

Eddie What? (*Into phone.*) Hang on, Dennis.

Miss Toner – wanted to know if he could huv 'a small advance' against his brother's estate until such time as he was able to . . .

Eddie (*overlapping*) Which Greek dive? (*Into phone.*) I hope you're listening to all this, Dennis. – Did he give you a number, Janice?

Miss Toner Yeah, five hundred quid. I just laughed.

Eddie A telephone number, ya stupid girl! Are you still there, Dennis? Hullo . . . Dennis? (*Slams down phone.*) Consider that Jubilee bonus of yours cancelled, Miss Toner.

Miss Toner What Jubilee bonus? A cassette of the Majestics' 'Greatest Hits'? I'd rather huv ma toenails individually prised off wi' a red hot paira tongs than huv ma ears polluted wi' that pile of keech, Mr Clockerty.

She grabs her coat, slips an arm into sleeve.

Eddie (*finding Dennis's number, redials*) As soon as I've got your redundancy money together you're fired, ma lady!

Miss Toner Aw, shuttup. (*Disappearing off.*)

Lights off. Total darkness.

Miss Toner 'Night, Mr Clockerty!

Eddie (*from blackout*) Bugger.

Lights up on Danny asleep in bathtub. Suzi appears, a housecoat over her pyjamas.

Suzi Right, McGlone, rise and shine!

Danny Waaah! Who's that? Where am I?

Suzi C'mon, move it! I've got my work to go to.

Danny (*struggling to his feet, wrapping quilt round him*) Remind me never to order Chicken Harry Lauder in a Greek taverna ever again . . . bwoop.

Suzi Get on with it, this chap'll be here in a minute!

Danny Ah, so thur is a '*chap*'? (*Steps onto floor.*) That's a relief. Thur's manys a doll can testify to the McGlones' 'animal magnetism' . . . Didny want to go thinkin' you wur the exception, Kettles . . . I mean, you urny a nun, right? (*Pause.*) You urny, ur you?

Suzi Take a look around you, McGlone . . . What d'you see?

Danny A very pleasant apartment. I'm glad I live here.

Suzi Like hell you do. What you see is one of everything: one chair, one plate, one cup, one toothbrush. Does that say anything to you?

Danny Yeah, it does. Look at the face. You thought I was goin' to be yur typical *insensitive* kinda guy that doesny pick up on stuff . . . Wrong again, Kettles. I know what one chair, one plate, one cup, one toothbrush means . . . yur skint, right?

Suzi It means I live alone, ya dooley . . . by myself, just me, on my own. Understand?

Danny What about this *chap* you jist mentioned?

Urgent ringing of doorbell. Suzi heads off to answer door.

Suzi This'll be him now. (*Disappearing off.*) He's just off the phone . . . something about a 'benefit gig'. Oh, yeah, and a 'contract'.

Danny What 'benefit gig'? What 'contract'?

Deranged doorbell ringing.

Suzi (*offstage*) I'm coming, dammit!

Lights up on Eddie poring over contract in his office.

Miss Toner He never went an' signed it, did he?

Eddie Of course he signed it, Miss Toner . . . (*Adding on extra pages.*) He just didn't sign all of it.

He proceeds to trace Danny's signature onto extra small-print pages.

Miss Toner You know you could get the jail fur that?

Eddie What, for correcting a clerical blunder? Surely not, Janice.

Phone rings. Miss Toner picks up receiver.

Miss Toner (*into phone*) Clockerty Enterprises . . .

Miss Toner *and* **Eddie** (*together*) . . . in association with Carntyne Promotions –

Miss Toner How might we assist you?

Eddie (*concentrating on forgery*) Well remembered, Miss T.

Miss Toner (*holding receiver out*) Vincent Diver . . . doesny sound too happy.

Eddie Tell him I'm away home.

Miss Toner Yuv just told him, Mr Clockerty.

Eddie looks up, discovers receiver next to his face. Takes it and covers mouthpiece. Miss Toner crosses to pour beverages.

Eddie You are on a verbal warning, m'girl.

Miss Toner Aye, that'll be right.

Eddie (*into phone*) Vincent, what a pleasant surprise . . . What can I do for you, old son? (*Crinkling paper into* *mouthpiece.*) I'm sorry, it's a very bad line. What was that? (*Hangs up.*)

Miss Toner (*putting mug on desk*) I've left the spoon in so you can howk out the lumpy milk.

Eddie Remind me, Janice, what time's this benefit gig at?

Lights up on Bomba, Fud and Danny doing 'Rock Around the Clock'. Dennis is positioned at door with bucket for 'donations'.

Vincent, his Gretch slung round his back, is in a clinch with Glenna in a dimly lit corner. As the number ends Bomba leaves his drumkit and has a peek into the bucket.

Dennis Well, thur's one thing fur sure, Big Theresa's no' gonny be givin' hurself brain damage tottin' that lot up.

Bomba That furst set was murder, Danny Boy. Who was it learnt you to sight-read, Stevie Wonder?

Danny Didny help matters wur lead guitar balin' out halfway through ma Little Richard medley . . . (*To Vincent, in clinch with Glenna.*) Ho, Diver! Put that pixie back on hur toadstool an' get yur broken-down butt back up here onstage where it belongs!

Fud Watch it, Danny Boy. You take on one Majestic, you take on all four – correction, *three* – right? (*To Vincent.*) C'mon, Lover Man, let the munchkin away to get on wi' hur homework!

Bomba (*getting back behind drums*) C'mon, you paira halfwits, cut the cackle, wuv got a gig to get on wi'!

Fud (*to Danny*) I'd've legged it fur the hills if I was you, that furst set was murder. Who was it learnt you to sight-read . . .

Bomba I've already done that one, O'Donnell.

Fud I wasny gonny do 'Stevie Wonder', I was gonny do Blind Lemon whatsisname . . .

Danny Jefferson.

Fud Thanks. (*To Bomba.*) See?

Vincent and Glenna break off their clinch.

Vincent God, talk about fickle? Yur jist after tellin' us last night it was better if we didny see one another unless it was absolutely . . . (*Sees look on Glenna's face.*) Aw, naw, don't tell me.

Glenna I'm afraid so, honey. I went to see the doctor this mornin' an' it's for definite this time.

Vincent (*shattered*) Aw, Glenna.

Glenna beams. Bomba, Fud and Danny lurch into desultory instrumental version of 'Rockin' Thru the Rye'. Eddie appears, looking pained.

Glenna Should you not be up there doin' the twiddly bits, Vincent?

Vincent Thur cried *riffs*, Glenna . . . an' aye, I should be.

Vincent makes his way zombie-like to the stage. Suzi appears just as Danny stoops to adjust his amp. Suzi looks around. Danny stands upright. Suzi spots him.

Suzi Danny?

Danny shades his eyes.

It's me . . . *Suzi!*

Danny Whoa . . . Kettles!

He roars straight into 'Tutti Frutti'. Fud and Bomba stare at one another. Vincent suddenly comes to life and hops onto the stage. The whole band rock'n'rolls into action. A great roar. Suzi jumps for joy. Danny exultant. Suzi turns away, suddenly not feeling so great . . .

And moves through to bathroom.

Danny How you doin', doll? You feelin' okay?

Suzi I'll be there in a second. (*Examines litmus strips from pregnancy testing kit.*)

Danny You know Glenna's goin', don't you?

Suzi What d'you mean, 'Glenna's going'? She's about fourteen. I thought he was married, this Vincent?

Danny He is married – to a Green Lady.

Danny appears. Suzi stuffs litmus strips into pocket and grabs a toothbrush.

Suzi Like in Tretchikoff, you mean?

Danny Like in District Nurse, stupit. She drives around rural Scotland in a Morris Minor with a boot-load of pills an' pamphlets showin' furst-time mothers how to fold nappies an' avoid it happenin' to them again.

Suzi What's he doing with a *girlfriend*, then? Or am I just being boringly 'Home Counties'?

Danny Naw, naw, I find the whole business morally reprehensible maself . . . Listen, about this upcomin' Silver Jubilee carry-on . . . ?

Suzi They're not going to let this Glenna out of school to go on a rock'n'roll tour, don't be daft, McGlone.

Danny I'm not talkin' about Glenna, I'm talkin' about you, Kettles . . . an' chuck referrin' to hur like she was in the Lower Thurd at St Trinian's, she's a grown wumman, the lassie. In fact, if you must know, she's an expectant mother.

Suzi The rotten sod . . . and his wife's supposed to be quite happy stuck at home looking after the kids, is that the idea?

Danny Huvny got any kids. Somethin' up wi' hur tubes, apparently. Or so Fud was saying.

Suzi I don't imagine Vincent's mentioned anything to her about Glenna tagging along, has he?

Danny Yuv got to be kiddin'. She'd kill him. An' if she ever finds out the doll's pregnant she'll kill the lot of us fur keepin' it dark.

Suzi So would I – you're a despicable bunch. Now, get out of here before I do you a serious mischief with the sharp end of this toothbrush!

She shoves Danny into the dark outside the bathroom. Takes litmus strips from dressing-gown pocket.

Danny C'mon, Kettles, what d'you say . . . you comin' or you not comin'?

Suzi (*in shock*) Oh, my God, I can't . . . I can't, Danny.

Danny 'Can't'? What d'you mean, '*can't*'? This thing is bigger 'n you an' me both an' that's sayin' somethin'! Can you no' see I'm crazy about you? C'mon, I'll give you a coaly-backie an' wull run away together . . . tie the knot, huv a squadda weans . . . What d'you say?

Suzi stares at the floor, paralysed.

(*Losing the rag.*) It wasny like this when the Flower of Scotland's Young Manhood was gettin' shipped out fur the Dardanelles. Even so-called Nice Girls wur happy to lay on a bitta farewell rumpy-pumpy!

Dennis Right, the Day of the Dead's over! Inty the wagon!

Lights up on Transit van, with Dennis at the wheel and Bomba, Fud and Vincent in the back. Danny chucks his bag in and climbs on board beside Dennis. Vincent swivels round to blow kisses and wave to Glenna, following behind in a Cortina.

Bomba (*eyes shut*) When're we gonny get there?

Dennis Oh, look, a tractor.

Fud Where?

Dennis Jist missed it . . . Okay, you guys, jist passin' Kirkcaldy on yur right. Next stop *Methil.*

Fud Hurray.

Danny (*checking rear-view mirror*) Mebbe shake hur off at the next roundabout, what d'you reckon?

Dennis (*shouting at another driver*) Aye, *and* you! Shake who off – the polis?

Danny Naw, the munchkin. (*Over his shoulder.*) What kinda transport's she got . . . a three-wheeler? Hur wee legs must be goin' like pistons.

Vincent is oblivious. More kisses and waving.

Fud Watch it, Danny Boy, you're still on probation, remember. She's drivin' Vinnie's Cortina.

Dennis You tell him, Francis. Aw, look, another tractor!

Fud *and* **Danny** (*together*) Where?

Vincent Wee burd spilled the beans about one of wur personnel gettin' wined an' dined by wur management last night to celebrate the launch of wur Silver Jubilee tour . . . Wasny you, was it, Bomba?

Bomba (*eyes still shut*) Yeah, that'll be the day.

Danny, Fud *and* **Dennis** (*together, sing*)
'Yeah, that'll be the day when you say goodbye,
Yeah, that'll be the day when you make me cry . . .
You say you're gonna leave me, you know it's a lie . . .'

Vincent What about you, O'Donnell?

Fud (*sings*)
'Yeah, that'll be the day-ay-ay when I die.'

The rest join in with an 'Ah-oooooh'.

Vincent Aw, I get it . . . (*Leaning forward, to Danny.*) So what was that in aid of? A pep talk on how to fill a dead man's shoes, was it?

Danny I hope yur no' talkin' to me, Diver.

Vincent 'Cos if it was, yur on a sticky wicket, pal!

Bomba, Fud *and* **Dennis** (*all at once, interjecting*) Behave yurself! / C'mon, Vinnie, huv less! / Ho, can it!

Vincent (*overlapping*) Bloody keyboards! Yur brother must be turnin' in his bloody grave right now!

Dennis (*shouting over Vincent*) If you must know, it was the wife an' I that Eddie was winin' an' dinin' last night!

Vincent What?

Bomba (*wide awake*) Who?

Fud Where?

Dennis Where what?

Fud Where was it he took youse?

Dennis Some Greek joint on the South Side . . . Yur never gonny believe what he ordered up fur us. *Kebabs.* Straight up, word of honour . . . *kebabs*!

Danny I wish you wouldny keep sayin' that . . . (*Blows nose loudly into hanky.*)

Dennis *Kebabs*, Vincent . . . you listenin'? That's what Eddie ordered up. *Kebabs,* yeah?

Vincent So? Big deal. (*Turning to look out back, showing off to Glenna.*)

Dennis *Kebabs!* You no' get it, naw?

Danny Gonny chuck sayin' that, Dennis?

Dennis Sayin' what?

Bomba (*coming to*) Sorry, did I hear somebody mention *kebabs*?

Dennis That's what Eddie ordered up fur the wife an' I last night . . . *kebabs*. No kiddin', Bomba.

Danny, at the end of his tether, buries his face in his hanky.

Bomba Aw, I thought you hud some in the wagon the way you wur talkin' . . . Huvny hud a *kebab* in God only knows how long. How's about you, Danny Boy? Fancy a *kebab* when you get there?

Dennis Wuv got here . . . everybody out!

Danny (*running off*) Aaaaaaaaaaaaaaaaargh!

Fud S'up wi' him?

Dennis Ho, c'mon, youse lot . . . yur bags! They're no' gonny turn up on the *carousel*!

Lights up on Eddie in shirtsleeves, tape measure round his neck. Miss Toner is sewing at a huge pair of silver lamé peg-bottoms.

Eddie (*to unseen Danny*) Walk this way again. That is stunning, Danny Boy . . . absolutely stunning. How are we progressing on the trouser front, Miss Toner?

Miss Toner I'm not workin' on the front, I'm workin' on the seat, is that not what you told me, Mr Clockerty?

Danny appears, bare-legged. He is wearing boxer shorts and big shoes with a roomy silver lamé stage suit jacket on.

Danny It's not that I don't appreciate it, Eddie, but it still feels kinda creepy.

Eddie Whereabouts . . . under the oxters?

Danny Naw, I mean wearin' somethin' that was intended fur . . . you know . . .?

Miss Toner A cadaver? Yeah, that's jist what I was thinkin'.

Danny Aye, thanks, sweetheart.

Eddie (*to Miss Toner*) What were we supposed to do, cut it up for hankies?

Miss Toner It wouldny make inty hankies, Mr Clockerty. Feel . . . it's like heavy-duty sandpaper.

Eddie (*making adjustments to Danny's jacket*) Don't pay any attention, Danny Boy, you're going to create a sensation when Dennis picks you up in that follow-spot this evening. Don't you think, Janice?

Miss Toner Yeah . . . like a big Thanksgivin' turkey wrapped up in Bacofoil. Here, stuff yur gams inty these. (*Chucks trousers at Danny.*) I'm away downstairs to the cocktail bar.

Eddie Miss Toner!

Lights up on Glenna and Vincent. A heavy silence.

Glenna Och, *I'll* go and ask!

Vincent (*grabbing her arm*) You do an' I'll . . .

He raises his fist.

Glenna You'll *what*?

Vincent lowers his fist, sticks his face close to hers.

Vincent I warned you that life on the road was gonny be tough, but you wouldny listen, would you? They don't start serving afternoon tea till four o'clock, *right*?

An angry and resentful silence. Fud and Bomba appear.

Fud Hi, Vinnie. Wuv jist ordered afternoon tea. (*To Glenna.*) D'you want a pokey-hat or somethin', doll?

Bomba (*to Vincent*) When is she off back to Glasgow? (*To Glenna.*) When you off back to Glasgow, sweetheart?

Glenna I'm goin' upstairs . . . Excuse me.

She teeters off.

Bomba Two hooses I can jist about take . . . Huvvin' a bit on the side I can turn a blind eye to, Vincent, but when you do the *real* durty on ma young sister that canny huv any kids . . .

Fud It's hur tubes.

Vincent Get stuffed, the pair of you.

Goes to push past. Bomba grabs his shirtfront.

Bomba Dump her, Vinnie.

Vincent Like hell I will. I asked hur to come on this tour an' she's comin' . . . all the way!

He brings his arm up, breaking Bomba's grip. Rattle of shirt buttons hitting the floor. Vincent looks down in horror.

Look what yuv done! Yuv tore aw the buttons off ma good shurt, ya cretinous tom-tom thumpin' bastart!

Bomba shoves his face into Vincent's.

Bomba Be warned, brother-in-law, next time it'll be somethin' else that gets tore off, you *dig*?

A few moments of high tension as this sinks in. Danny jumps into the light in the silver lamé suit.

Danny (*sings*)
'Ah-well, it's one for the money,
Two for the show,
Three to get ready, now . . .'

(*Stops dead.*) Aw, er . . . Hi, you cats, jist wonderin' if thur was any afternoon tea on the go?

Bomba and Fud take an arm each and escort Danny out. Vincent is left pondering his immediate future.

Glenna sneaks back in, comes up behind Vincent.

Glenna Boo!

She laughs as Vincent almost dies.

I snuck back down to drag you upstairs, for a very special treat . . .

Vincent Naw, I canny, babe. You don't know what Clockerty's like if I'm not there to oversee wur every what-d'you-cry-it . . .

Glenna (*leading him away*) Sound-check? I know. This's just your appetiser . . . the main course comes later . . . After the gig . . . when you'll be *really* hungry.

Vincent I'm pretty peckish the now . . . C'mon.

They head off to go upstairs.

So, that's it settled. Soon as wuv hud wur puddin' yur goin' back to Glasgow, right?

Glenna I'm *what*?

Vincent (*offstage*) Is that not what we agreed, doll?

Offstage screams, thumps and yelps.

Lights up on Danny at payphone. He puts the receiver to his ear.

Danny Please, God, please God, jist make hur pick up the phone an' I swear on ma dead brother's grave I'll turn over a new leaf. (*Shoves coin into slot.*) I'll no' even curse or nuthin' . . . (*Listens.*) Aw, bugger! *(Slams phone down on his knuckles.*) Oooow!

Lights up on sound-check. Dennis does the rounds of equipment while Fud and Bomba noodle on bass and drums. Vincent's guitar sits on its stand.

Fud Mebbe him an' the munchkin's absconded, naw?

Dennis Cortina's still in the hotel car park.

Danny appears.

Danny How come wur waitin' fur Diver anyhow? (*Runs fingers over silent keyboard.*) Has he got the batteries fur this contraption in his pocket or somethin'?

Bomba Tell him, Francis.

Fud Disny take batteries, Danny Boy, you jist plug it straight inty the mains.

Bomba Tell him about the Majestics' protocol, ya dummy.

Fud Aw, that? Sure. See, the thing is, Danny Boy, thur's certain band rules an' traditions that huv to be observed, otherwise . . . (*To Bomba.*) Otherwise what?

Bomba Otherwise *anarchy* sets in, an' when anarchy sets in . . .

Bomba, Fud *and* **Dennis** (*together*) Rock'n'roll goes down the toilet.

Danny Well, in view of the fact that wur lead guitar-picker isny here when he's meant to be an' that yours truly's already hud four trips to that *same* toilet on account of how it's his furst gig in front of a paying audience an' he's got a really bad dose of the skitters, might I humbly suggest that *anarchy* is a viable option in the circumstances? Hands up who votes furra talk wi' Eddie? (*Sticks his hand in the air.*)

Fud Furget it, Danny Boy, Eddie's only gonny put the blame onty Wee Tommy Cairns fur whatever it is wur complainin' about.

Dennis He's still puttin' the blame onty Wee Tommy fur the band's one an' only hit single.

Danny What – fur the fact it was thur one an' only or . . .?

Fud Naw, fur the fact that it would've went further up the charts if Wee Tommy hudny made a blunder an' purchased all of his copies from the one record shop.

Danny Hang on a minute, ur you tellin' me that . . .?

Dennis Jist wasny enough mugs – sorry, record buyers – goin' out thur way to snap up the Majestics' debut 45 fur to punt it inty the Hit Parade, so what Eddie an' Wee Tommy done was . . .

Danny C'mon, you guys, you don't huv to be a *News of the World* hack to recognise a straightforward piece of criminal jiggery-pokery when you come across it.

Fud Set Wee Tommy back about four an' a half grand.

Danny Set me back more'n that, I don't mind tellin' you. 'Scuse me while I make yet another trip to the toilet – vomitorium section. (*Hurries off, hand over his mouth.*)

Lights up on Vincent heading for sound-check. The payphone rings as he walks past.

Vincent (*snatching receiver, into phone*) East Fife Animal Welfare Centre. All the animals've been put down so thur's nobody here to take yur call, but if you'd like to . . . Sorry, give who a message? Aw, him . . . Aye, if I see him. What'd you say yur name was again? (*Snorts.*) Sure, yeah, I'll tell him you rang . . . (*Goes to hang up, changes his mind.*) Hey, listen, Suzi . . . hus anybody ever told you what a sexy number you sound over the telephone? (*Holds receiver away from his ear, then slams it down.*) Dolls? Who needs them? (*Loudly.*) Awright, I'm here. What are we waitin' fur?

As Vincent joins the sound-check, Danny comes racing back on.

Danny Ten pee, ten pee, ten pee, ten pee, please, God, please, God, this time . . . this time . . . (*Rams 10p into payphone, dials.*) This time, pleeeeeeeeeease!

Dennis appears at Danny's side and grabs his arm.

Dennis C'mon, Danny Boy, yur on!

Suzi (*voice on dangling payphone*) Hullo? Is that you, Danny? Hullo?

An offstage wail from Danny as Dennis and he disappear off.

The opening bars to 'Promised Land'. Lights up on 'live footage' of the Majestics, circa 1964, performing one of their most popular numbers, with silver-suited Danny playing Big Jazza, Fender Strat strapped to his ample frame, on vocals.

Blackout.

Lights up on Sheena Fisher at scene of Big Jazza's fatal crash. Camera and Director/Soundman filming her report.

Sheena A rare clip of the Majestics performing live back in 1964. They looked pretty much unstoppable then, but it was here in this Glasgow street just a few weeks ago that Jazza McGlone, nicknamed 'The Beast of Rock' by the Scottish tabloids, discovered the hard way that performing *live* was no longer on his list of fun things to do alongside his gargantuan appetite for booze, drugs and women, when the Ford Sierra he was driving ploughed headlong into this bus shelter behind me at over ninety miles per . . . (*Turning to take in bus shelter.*) Dammit . . . Sorry, Duggie, some idiot's moved the bloody bus shelter.

Director Cut!

Lights up on Danny, Suzi and Dennis – Danny in tartan zoot suit, Suzi in something less roary but equally eye-catching.

Suzi What're you talking about, McGlone, I did so phone . . . weeks and weeks ago . . . Whoever it was that picked up promised to pass on the message. You never phoned me back!

Danny I'm forever phonin' you! The furst time I've found you was fifteen minutes ago. I've phoned you from Faifley, Fife, Fort William, Forres, Fochabers, an' jist last Friday from a phonebox in Forfar, I was that frantic . . . an' guess what? You wur engaged! Fur the forty-seventh time in four weeks! By the time I'd found another fifty pee fur to phone you again, the door was flung open an' I was frog-marched to Fat Sam's an' forced to perform fourteen numbers, includin' 'The Phantom of the

Fillmore' in front of four hundred of the faithful 'fore they'd hud enough an' started flingin' beer cans fulla you-know-what . . . Never phoned you back?

Dennis appears.

Dennis Right, Danny Boy, let's find these people, I'm parked on a double yella line. (*To Passerby.*) 'Scuse me, Jim, any idea where we can locate a badly buckled bus shelter in this particular neighbourhood?

Passerby Thur aw pretty badly buckled aboot here, pal, but thur's a particularly badly buckled wan back there aways. Canny miss it.

He heads off.

Danny Yes, very droll . . . cheers.

Suzi Oh, look – there's what's-her-face. (*Waving.*) Pain-in-the-bum I was at school with. Wonder what she's doing in this neck of the woods?

Danny Yo . . . Sheena Fisher! Danny McGlone . . . Beast of Rock's young scud, ready fur wardrobe an' make-up!

Suzi What?

Lights up on Manhattan Casuals. Eddie is holding up a T-shirt with Danny's face on the front and the legend TWENTY-FIVE YEARS YOUNG AND STILL ROYALLY ROCKIN'! *on the back. He turns it this way and that: one sleeve is noticeably longer than the other.*

Eddie Well?

Miss Toner Er . . .

Eddie Oh for pity's sake, Janice, can't you see what's up with this garment?

Miss Toner Chuck bawlin' at us, I'm lookin' at it!

Eddie
Clockerty

Eddie Look harder then! If I'm going to lodge a complaint in the strongest possible terms with Thomas Cairns Esquire's Personalised T-Shirt and Sloppy Joe Department I'd like my staff to be a hundred per cent . . .

Miss Toner (*interrupting*) Ah . . . jist twigged, Mr Clockerty. Trades Descriptions Act, right?

Eddie Precisely. Now, away up the stair and get me Wee Tommy on the blower.

Miss Toner What it should say on the back is 'Seventy-Five Years of the Same Old Junk and Jist About to Peg Out – This's Yur Last Chance to Catch Them Before They Die'.

Eddie Take my tip, Miss Toner, that sort of attitude won't get you very far up the almost-brand-new-slightly-shop-soiled-but-otherwise-perfect garment industry stepladder. I'll get ahold of the wee bugger myself!

Lights up on Fud and Vincent. Vincent is righteously agitated.

Vincent So if thur no' here where the bloody hell ur they? Did you manage to get through to Eddie?

Fud Him an' Wee Tommy wur huvin' a workin' brunch so I hudda word wi' Janice. Know what they went back to Glasgow fur? To make a TV movie . . . all about Danny Boy. (*Seeing Vincent's face.*) I know . . . I hud the same reaction. Thuv stuck his kisser onty a whole loada T-shurts fur to advertise it . . . Away an' phone hur yurself if you don't believe me.

Vincent She's pullin' yur leg, O'Donnell.

Fud Didny sound like she was pullin' anybody's leg, Vinnie.

Vincent *I'll* talk to hur.

Fud Good. (*As Vincent heads off.*) Only don't say who it was that told you!

Lights up on Eddie at his desk, while telephone rings and goes on ringing.

Eddie It's Vincent . . . I *know* it's Vincent. Any sensible person would've rung off by now.

Miss Toner Let me get it . . . I'll tell him the T-shurts are on thur way to the Thurd World, okay?

Reaches for telephone. Eddie prevents her from picking up.

Eddie And how d'you explain about young Danny and the TV programme, Miss Smartypants?

Miss Toner Don't be daft, thur all goin' to see it when it goes out. Besides, I just overheard you tellin' that wee creep Cairns that they wur all goin' to be featured, the whole band, so what's the beef?

Eddie What's the beef? The beef is that while Danny Boy is going out in glorious Technicolor, the other band members plus their late singer will only make a fleeting appearance on scratchy eight-mil black-and-white captured by *Mrs* Clockerty from the wallbars of a TA drill hall in Coatbridge on a four-quid home movie camera twenty years back – that's the beef, Miss Toner!

Miss Toner Aw.

Eddie 'Archive footage' . . . that's what you overheard me telling Wee Tommy. 'Archive footage', right?

Miss Toner I'm a Drapery Assistant, Mr Clockerty, not the Cambridge Street Film Buff of the Year! As far as I'm concerned, 'archive footage' could jist as well be them secondhand blue suede bumpers wur sellin' in the shop down the stair!

Eddie Shhh . . . listen!

Miss Toner Listen what?

The telephone has stopped ringing.

Eddie Is that a good sign or a bad sign, d'you think?

Miss Toner You don't pay me nearly enough to think. Work it out fur yurself, I'm away to do ma nails. (*She heads off.*)

Eddie Get you back here this instant, d'you hear me? (*As Miss Toner disappears.*) *Janice!*

Lights up on Danny, the worse for drink and stretched out on the sofa in Suzi's apartment. He is gazing blearily up at the ceiling.

Danny (*loudly*) Don't know if yur aware of it, Kettles, but thur's a damp patch on yur ceilin' that's a dead ringer fur the Vurjin Mary. (*Sitting up for a closer inspection of the 'image'.*) Naw, as you were, it's the other one . . . Big Theresa. Nup, wrong again. . . . it's the Big Bopper. (*Sings.*) 'Chantilly lace an' a pretty face, an' a pony tail hangin' down . . .'

Suzi appears with mug.

Suzi Black coffee.

Danny Yur a chum, Kettles. (*Takes coffee.*)

Suzi And you, McGlone, are an idiot. By the time I left you and Barbie Doll Fisher to it I could tell there was no way this TV *documentary* was shaping up to be the 'glowing testimonial' to the musical talents of the Majestics your management was trumpeting.

Danny 'Tumpurting'? Did you say 'tumpurt' – God, I canny even say it – 'tumpurting'?

Suzi What the hell were you playing at? He was *your* brother. *She* gets paid to do a hatchet job, *you* don't, so what in the name of God were you celebrating?

Danny 'Tumpurting' . . .

Doorbell goes.

Suzi That'll be Dennis . . . Get that coffee down your stupid neck, get those togs off and get under the shower.

Doorbell goes again.

All right, all right, we hear you! (*As she goes, to Danny.*) There's no hot water left, by the way, so be warned.

Danny 'No hot water' . . . check. 'Tum-pur-ting' . . .

He disappears off as Suzi reappears with Dennis in tow.

Suzi (*to Dennis*) It'll take me two minutes to pack a bag, I'm coming with you . . . I don't trust that big . . .

Danny (*offstage*) *Bugger!* Waaaaaaaaaaaaaah!

Lights up on Eddie at his desk. Loud banging at shop door. Eddie looks up from his papers.

Vincent (*offstage*) Open up, d'you hear me?

More banging and door-rattling. Eddie gets up and grabs his coat.

(*Offstage.*) I've drove aw the way from Ardrossan wi' a pregnant vocalist in the motor, I know yur up there in yur hidey-hole, ya midden!

More banging and door-rattling.

Awright, if that's how you want to play it!

A lengthy silence. Eddie gets down on his hands and knees and hides under his desk.

The sound of running footsteps. A pause, followed by an almighty crash of shattering glass, a piercing scream from Glenna dueting with Vincent's demented howling. Vincent explodes head-over-heels into view, clutching his bloody napper, and ends up face to face with Eddie under the desk.

Eddie (*peeping out*) Oh, it's you, Vincent. Why didn't you just pick up the phone?

Glenna comes rushing in from the street as Miss Toner appears, having just varnished her nails.

Glenna Aw my God, look at yur head!

Vincent (*reeling to his feet*) Right, ya bastart!

Eddie takes to his heels pursued by an irate Vincent, hampered somewhat by his injury.

Miss Toner (*waving her hands about to dry her nails*) Hoi, chuck that! Yur gettin' blood all over ma good shorthand notebook!

Vincent (*to Eddie, playing cat and mouse with him*) C'mere, ya midden, you've got a lotta explainin' to do! Grab ahold of him, Glenna!

Glenna (*grabbing Vincent*) C'mon, you, get back inty that motor car, you're meant to be on stage at Ardrossan in twenty-five minutes!

Vincent (*holding on to Eddie*) Right, ya midden, inty the motor!

Eddie Janice!

Miss Toner I'm right at yur back, Mr Clockerty . . . (*Piling into back seat.*) D'you need a bandage for that?

She swipes Eddie's white silk scarf and passes it to Vincent, who is getting into the passenger seat, with Glenna behind the wheel.

Vincent Right, go, Glenna, go!

Glenna (*crashing through gears*) I'm goin', I'm goin'! (*Bursting into song.*) 'Born to be wild . . .'

Vincent (*to Eddie and Miss Toner*) C'mon, sing up!

Eddie *and* **Miss Toner** (*together, singing*) 'Born to be wild . . .'

Glenna 'Born to be wild . . .'

Eddie (*leaning forward, to Glenna*) It's not that I'm not enjoying myself but d'you think you could keep your eyes on . . .?

Glenna (*turning her head, overlapping*) Don't talk to me while I'm driving! Right, *everybody*! 'Born to be wild . . .'

Miss Toner Aw, my God, watch out fur that . . .

Blackout.

Vincent, Eddie *and* **Glenna** Waaaaaaaaaaaaaaaaaah . . .

Lights up on Suzi, Dennis and Danny, newly arrived at their Ardrossan B&B. Dennis is loaded down with Suzi's luggage, Danny hungover.

Danny Gonny give it a by, Kettles? The only untoward incident I witnessed on the drive back from Glasgow was a pink elephant ridin' pillion on a moped comin' through Bridge of Weir. God, ma napper . . .

Suzi (*to Dennis*) *You* must've seen it, you were driving!

Dennis Pink elephant on a moped? Canny say I noticed, sweetheart. (*Dumps all of Suzi's bags.*) Room Six . . . breakfast between seven an' seven-thurty. Y'there, Vinnie?

He disappears off.

Suzi The Cortina that shot out of that side road!

Dennis (*offstage, sings*) 'Born to be wild . . .' Y'there, Mr Diver?

Suzi You *must've* seen it, McGlone, you were sitting in the passenger seat . . . I just caught a glimpse of the chap in the funny hat's face as their car went off the road into that field . . .

Dennis (*reappearing with Vincent's stage suit*) Didny come through this way, did he?

Suzi (*to Danny*) You absolutely positive you didn't see anything?

Dennis (*disappearing off*) Vincent?

Danny Gonny chuck shoutin' at us, Kettles? I'm beginnin' to wish I hudny brung you now!

Suzi God, listen to it! You didn't *bring* me, I took time off work to keep tabs on you on this tour so you don't end up making a complete idiot of yourself with some other . . . (*Biting her tongue.*)

Danny Aha! So that's it!

Suzi What?

Danny Yur jealous!

Suzi Me? Jealous? Don't make me laugh, McGlone. Me? (*Starts laughing, stops.*) D'you know how many O levels she got?

Danny Who's this wur talkin' about?

Suzi *Two*. One in 'Treachery' and the other one in 'Eye Make-up and Mascara'!

She disappears off, dragging her luggage.

Blackout.

Danny (*from blackout*) Ha! Knew it! You ur so jealous! Yaaaahoo!

Lights up on Sheena Fisher and Director.

Sheena Let's run it again, Duggie.

Director hits 'Rewind' then 'Play'.

Danny (*on screen*) I was jist a kid at the time, swaggering about the school playground goin', 'Ma big bree's in the Top Twenty,' so you can imagine how I felt when I discovered that Eddie Clockerty an' this other slimeball actually *finagled* thur single inty the charts all them years ago. It was like findin' out that Hans Christian Andersen was a werewolf . . . or the Pope was a drag queen . . . An' that isny the worst of it. You know what else Clockerty an' his scumbag cohort got up to . . .? Yur no' gonny believe this. They put a *contract* out on aw the rival bands in Glasgow. Got a big guy from Feegie to pay them a visit . . . smashed aw thur guitar players' fingers wi' a heavy hammer an' got thur lead singers to gargle wi' ammonia – that's how come the Majestics cornered all the ballroom gigs . . . An' that's not to mention how they got the band onty *Ready Steady Go*, that's a book in itself. An' it isny one you want to read yur weans at bedtime either . . . Hang on, where's Kettles off to? Ho, come back, Suzi . . . me an' Sheena's jist huvvin' a chinwag while the camera boy's swappin' lenses . . . (*to camera/ Sheena*) So, what was she like at school, then? She said you wur an absolute . . .

Screen goes blank.

Director Nice work, Sheena. We can lop that end bit off and make it look like he's perfectly aware he's talking directly to camera.

Sheena They say that confession's good for the soul. We've done that big mug a favour.

Director (*as Sheena heads off*) That manager of theirs once sold me a Billy Eckstein shirt . . . 'Wash like a hanky,' he said. I hope you nail the bastard.

Sheena It'll be a pleasure.

She disappears off.

Director 'Night, gorgeous.

Blackout.

Lights up slowly on Eddie and Miss Toner by the roadside – frozen.

Miss Toner So how come it was *that* pair that got rushed off to the nearest infirmary, an' you an' me has to hang about in the middle of nowhere makin' sure that nobody drives off in that clapped-out wreck of Diver's? I mean, it's not like it's got enough wheels left to go anywhere. (*Sniffs.*) What's that funny smell? Huv you been rubbin' that stuff inty yur scalp again, Mr Clockerty?

Eddie You're in the country, Miss Toner.

Miss Toner Naw, that *other* funny smell. D'you not . . .?

A loud 'whump'. Eddie and Miss Toner are brilliantly illuminated for a second as the unseen Cortina explodes in flames.

Eddie *and* **Miss Toner** (*together*) Aaaaaaaaaaaaargh!

Lights up on Fud and Bomba backstage at Club Paradiso. Bomba is agitated. Dennis appears with Vincent's stage suit on a hanger.

Dennis Jist been to huv a pow-wow wi' the boy on the door wi' 'I Belong to Glasgow' tattooed on his forehead.

Bomba And?

Dennis (*hanging suit up*) He says if thur isny four Majestics onstage by the time he's let aw the punters in, the lot of us ur gonny get kneecapped.

Fud *Kneecapped?*

Danny stumbles in, still shaky from aftermath of drinking.

Dennis An' that includes you, Danny Boy.

Danny What does? Diver no' here yet, naw?

Lights up on Glenna in hospital bed, Vincent at her bedside.

Glenna I'm fine, Vincent, they're only keeping me in overnight for observation . . . you better go.

Vincent, his head swathed in bandages, leans down and kisses her.

Vincent As long as yur sure yur okay?

Glenna I love you, Vincent.

Vincent I love me too, Glenna.

Glenna (*giggling*) Go . . . you'll be late!

Vincent You look after yurself 'cos I want you up there beside me at wur next gig. I've arranged a meetin' wi' Eddie about it.

Blows her a kiss and is gone.

(*Offstage.*) Somebody get us a taxi. Ardrossan, Club Paradiso – *now*!

Lights up on the Majestics onstage at the Club Paradiso, as they launch into 'That'll Be the Day' with Danny on vocals. They are in great form – it is only when 'Vincent' steps up to join Danny in a duet that we see that it is Suzi. She steps away from the mike and into a guitar solo of some considerable verve and originality.

Blackout.

Lights up on Vincent pacing the floor of the Ardrossan digs – seething.

Noisy and high-spirited arrival of Bomba, Fud, Danny and Suzi offstage. Fud and Bomba tumble on, laughing. They spot Vincent and fall silent.

Bomba Bloody hell . . .

Fud What happened to *you*, Vinnie?

Vincent I've jist came from the hospital.

Danny appears with a fish supper in his hand.

Danny What was it, a frontal lobotomy?

Suzi (*offstage*) You there, Danny? (*She appears, spots Vincent.*) Oh my God, it's the chap in the funny hat that was sitting next to the driver of the Cortina that went off the road into a field –

Vincent Hang about, that's *ma* stage gear . . .

Suzi – except I can see now it's that rotten sod Diver and it's not a hat, it's a bandage.

Danny Dead ringer fur Daffy Duck, don't you think?

Vincent What's this burd doin' wearin' ma stage gear? Eh?

Suzi Were the other people in the car okay?

Dennis appears. Vincent rounds on him.

Vincent C'mere, you . . . What's this burd wearin' ma' bloody stage gear fur?

Suzi (*to Dennis*) You know that dark-blue Cortina you never noticed coming the wrong way round that Keep Left sign . . .?

Vincent (*overlapping*) Naw, stop, stop, furst things furst! How come you're strollin' about in ma bloody stage gear, whoever you ur?

Fud Steady, Vinnie, it was either that ur me, Bomba, Danny Boy an' Dennis there gettin' wurselves kneecapped.

Vincent Kneecapped?

Bomba Which is how come the burd there hud to go onstage.

Vincent What d'you mean, 'onst—'? Ur you tellin' me that hur there – an actual *burd* – was onstage wi' the Majestics playin' lead guitar the night?

Fud *And* vocalisin'.

Vincent *What?*

Bomba Wasny aw that bad either, Vinnie.

Vincent Hold it right there . . . I know I'm hallucinatin' but lemme get this straight. This burd, this doll, this . . . *chick* . . . upon whose features I huvny clapped eyes until a coupla seconds ago, hus been onstage wi' *ma* band, in *ma* suit, playin' *ma* guitar, an' fur all I know, singin' all of *ma* numbers wi' the Apprentice Boy from NewYork who, as far as I'm concerned, husny passed thon audition we hud at Big Theresa's benefit do, while the greatest young female rock vocalist since Janis bloody Joplin, that you wouldny huv in the Majestics fur love nur money, is lyin' in a hospital bed right now, miles from anywhere, 'under observation' . . . Naw, listen, listen! The reason she's lyin' in a hospital bed miles from anywhere 'under observation' right now isny anythin' to do wi' hur huvvin' ma kid but everythin' to do wi' that clown there . . . (*Pointing at Dennis.*) Aye, *you*! I thought I was seein' things, but the burd in ma stage gear there jist confirmed fur us that it was you right enough, wur bloody *road manager*, that ran ma bloody Cortina off the highway an' upside down inty a bloody tatty field as we wur racin' hell fur leather through here wi' Eddie Clockerty in the back seat dolin' out 'drivin' lessons' to a doll that's only jist passed hur test last week an' the only reason that *she's* drivin' an' not *me* is because I'm sittin' beside hur in the passenger seat wi' a suspected fractured skull from huvvin' to drop everythin' includin' wur sound-check in order to belt back to Glasgow an' chin Clockerty Enterprises on behalf of *youse* two about this bloody TV movie that *he's* in that Eddie husny saw fit to let onty *me* about, an' what do I get? Naw, naw, I'll tell you what I get . . . I get shafted, that's what I get! Betrayed, ridiculed, seriously injured an' *shafted*!

Danny C'mon, *Daffy*, it wasny like that . . . (*Proffering fish supper.*) Here, help yurself to some chips.

Vincent (*throwing his head back*) Waaaaaaa – (*Checks himself.*) Good Christ . . . *Noreen*.

All heads turn to look as Noreen, in District Nurse's uniform and with a small overnight bag in her hand, appears.

Vincent What the hell're you doin' here?

Noreen Why the hell shouldn't I be here? I'm your wife, yes? Why aren't the rest of them in fancy dress? Or is this just you showing off as usual? Here, you can show me to our room. (*Hands her bag to Vincent.*) And get that silly bunnet off, you'll look for all the world like Daffy bloody Duck.

She reaches up and gives Vincent's 'silly bunnet' a sharp tug. A collective gasp of horror goes up as she realises too late what she's done. All the others leave them to it and sneak off.

The look on Vincent's face is a picture – as Noreen lets go, Vincent drops into a crouch, his hands hovering around his injured head.

Vincent Ah . . . ah . . . ah . . . ah . . . aaaaaaaaaaaaya! Stupit-bloody-bitch-that-you-are-yuv-made-it-even-bloody-worse'n-it-was-before!

Noreen Come on, darlin', let me help you. *I'll* find our room. I can't tell you how much I've missed you. I know it was a surprise, but I couldn't wait to see you . . . to put my arms around you . . . Oh, Vincent . . . Vincent . . .

Vincent (*as he is helped up*) It's Room Five . . . Ahyah . . .

They disappear off.

Lights up on Glenna propped up in bed, deathly pale.

Nurse appears – consults Glenna's chart and moves round bed to check her pulse.

An unkempt and haggard Vincent comes round the screen: a plaster has replaced the bandage on his head. The Nurse gives him a withering look.

Vincent How is she?

Nurse She's been asking every half an hour when you were coming to see her – it's been three days now.

Vincent Wur tour's moved up north to Buckie . . . Deep Sea Ballroom. Standin' room only. How we doin', doll? Sorry I never got here yesterday.

Glenna (*smiling weakly*) Or the day before.

Vincent Or the day before that even, I know, I know . . . wasny anywhere near a phone either. See, the thing is . . .

He gives Nurse 'a look'. Nurse takes the hint and disappears off.

Glenna It's all right, I know what you're goin' to tell me.

Vincent I'm still in shock, no kiddin'. She turned up in Ardrossan out the blue an' followed me up to Buckie.

Glenna I hope you an' hur haven't . . .?

Vincent C'mon, doll, I was *numb* . . . *concussed*. I could hardly even walk, never mind . . .

Glenna Promise me one thing, Vincent.

Vincent Sure, babe, anythin'.

Glenna Promise me you willny sleep with hur . . . in Buckie or anywhere else.

Vincent Aw, fur God's sake, huvva heart, Glenna . . . She's ma wife, fur cryin' out loud!

Glenna *Exactly* – now, promise me!

Nurse sweeps back in.

Vincent (*hurriedly*) Awright, awright, I promise. (*To Nurse.*) It's okay, I'm gettin' out yur road . . . Took us four an' a quarter hours to get here from Buckie an' by the time I get back to bloody Buckie I might jist make it fur the sound-check. (*To Glenna.*) See an' you do as yur told, d'you hear me? I want you back on yur pins an' beltin' out 'Be-bop-a-Lula' wi' me an' the other two at that Pavilion gig in wur home city, yeah? (*To Nurse.*) I do a lotta work fur one of the musical charities . . . You take good care of this doll an' this joint could be in line fur an illuminated citation . . . Mother Teresa's already got hurs. (*Blowing kiss to Glenna.*) See you, babe.

He disappears off behind screen.

Nurse Time for your afternoon nap, Mrs Diver. (*Makes Glenna comfortable.*) I trust that was him promising to make the effort in future?

Glenna Yeah, something like that.

Nurse You're not at all well, you know.

Glenna I'll just have to make myself well then, won't I? And it's not 'Mrs Diver' . . .

Nurse I beg your pardon?

Glenna . . . at least, not *yet*.

Lights up on Vincent, Fud, Bomba and Danny onstage at Buckie. Suzi on sidelines.

Danny (*watching Suzi, sings*)
'Dream . . . dream, dream, dream . . .
When I want you in my arms . . .
When I want you and all your charms . . .
Whenever I want you, all I have to do
Is dream . . . dream, dream, dream . . .'

Lights up on Glenna, dressed for sneaking out of hospital against medical advice. She packs all her stuff (including lumberjacket knitted in blue and pink baby wool) into plastic bags.

Glenna (*sings*)
'I can make you mine, taste your lips of wine . . .
Any time, night or day . . .'

Lights up on Noreen in Buckie hotel room in a new nightdress, turning this way and that in mirror.

Glenna *and* **Noreen** (*together, sing*)
'Only trouble is, gee whizz,
I'm dreamin' ma life away . . .'

Vincent steps up to take guitar solo. Danny watches a preoccupied Suzi. Glenna and Noreen put on their make-up.

Danny, Glenna, Noreen *and* **Suzi** (*together, sing*)
'Dream . . . dream, dream, dream . . .
When I want you in my arms . . .
When I want you and all your charms . . .
Whenever I want you, all I have to do
Is dream . . . dream, dream, dream . . . dream.'

Lights up on Radio Buckie – Bomba and Danny wearing shades and badly hungover while Dennis leafs idly through a copy of Rolling Stone.

The DJ Lachie, in cowboy shirt, baseball cap and kilt, sits at a desk. He slips his headphones back on and leans in to mike.

Lachie And a more beautiful and haunting way to wake up and smell the coffee I can't imagine. (*Loudly.*) You're tuned to Radio Buckie, the thinking loon's Radio Ga-Ga, two-two-nine metres on the medium wave . . . (*Punches up heavy metal Strathspey station ident.*) Six short minutes after the big hour of six here on the *Breakfast Show* phone-in . . . (*Punches up phone-in jingle.*) Your old pal Wacky Lachie in the Radio Buckie hot seat thru till eight! (*Another burst of Strathspey.*) And, as promised in the run-up to the *Breakfast Show*, I'm joined by two great mates of mine from the Majestics . . . currently on tour in and around Wonderful Radio Buckieland all this week. A big, big welcome to the phone-in show, Danny and Bambi! (*Punches up fanfare. Dennis leans in for a word.*) And it's a smacked botty and sent to bed without any cocoa there from the band's roadie for getting *Bomba's* name confused with the little babby deer from the old Disney cartoon weepie. (*To Dennis.*) Cheers, Dunky. And here's a wee taster from the band's Golden Jubilee tour showreel . . . Fasten your seatbelts and get a good grip of the kitchen table for 'Runaway'.

Punches up the Majestics' version of Del Shannon's 'Runaway'.

Lights up on Suzi's hotel room. Suzi in dressing gown. The Majestics on radio. Fud appears.

Fud Don't mind if I join you, naw? Huvny gave us a wireless in ma room . . . Cheers. (*Makes himself comfy.*)

Suzi Make yourself at home . . . 'Scuse me, you're sitting on my toilet bag. (*Extricates it from under him.*) *Cheers.*

Lights up on Noreen and Vincent, Vincent in leopardskin Y-fronts, Noreen in dressing gown over newly purchased 'alluring underwear'.

Vincent Yak-yak-yackitty-yak . . . Chuck goin' on at us, yur doin' ma napper in, Noreen! An' where the hell're aw ma clean shurts? Look at these, thur mockit!

Noreen And whose fault is that? What d'you need a clean shirt for anyhow? It's ten past six in the bloody morning!

Vincent I know it's ten past six in the bloody mornin', an' you know how I know? 'Cos that's when you normally start gettin' tore inty me!

Noreen There's some new tart, isn't there? Isn't there? Only this one's different, isn't she? She can't be all that different, can she? From me? Vincent . . . darling?

She opens her dressing gown.

Vincent Fur God's sake, cover yurself up! You look like some long-past-thur-sell-by-date old whore floggin' condemned meat in that get-up!

He takes a swig from a half-bottle of whisky.

Lights up on Suzi's room, Suzi exasperated. A knock.

Suzi (*to Fud*) I hope this's for you . . . It's open!

Noreen appears in dressing gown – Vincent's dirty shirts in her hand, hair all over the place. She spots Fud.

Noreen Oh, sorry, I didn't realise . . .

Fud Hi, Noreen hen.

Suzi (*to Noreen*) No, no, it's not like that . . . Come in, he's just going.

Fud 'S that a new hairdo yuv got?

Suzi Do you mind?

Fud Naw, she suits it. (*To Noreen.*) You mebbe want them to touch in yur roots, but otherwise . . . Awright, awright, I'm goin'. (*Gets himself upright.*) Can I get a lenna yur wireless? Naw, stupit idea . . . (*Heading off.*) Not even got a socket in ma bloody room. Catch you later, Noreen hen . . . (*Pause before leaving.*) Really dig that new hairdo.

He disappears off. Noreen slumps down onto bed.

Suzi There . . . Lemme make you a cup of tea and we can swap notes, yeah?

Fade song on radio.

Lachie . . . And I do believe we have our first caller on the line . . .

Lights up on Radio Buckie studio.

You're through to Danny and Bomba . . . go ahead, caller.

The amplified voice is young, female and local.

Caller I'd like to ask Bomba MacAteer something.

Lachie And your name is?

Caller D'you remember the last time the Majestics played Buckie?

Danny Aye, they lost four–nothin', sweetheart.

Bomba Sure do, doll . . . It was summer 1964 . . . Thur was us, Them, The Who, an' what's-his-name –

Danny Al Jolson.

Bomba (*clamping hand over Danny's mouth*) – the boy Pitney.

Interference on amplified phone line.

Lachie Okay, we seem to have lost our first caller, so let's go to line two. Are you there, line two?

Caller It's still me, and I'm looking at a big autographed photy of Bomba and a whole lotty other folk and ma mum's there and she looks that young-looking and she's cutting a sorty cake . . .

Bomba I can tell you exactly where that is, sweetheart. Back room at the British Legion . . . Vincent's burthday party. The whole lot of us includin' wur management got absolutely slaughtered that night . . .

Lachie (*punching up drunken bagpipes*) So there you go, a young lady with a fascinating souvenir of the Majestics' first visit to the North-East . . . and just before we go back onto the phone lines for another call I'd like to take a moment here – (*Cues in syrupy muzak.*) – to pay our own Very Special Radio Buckie Tribute to a Living Legend . . . the late, great Big Jazza McGlone, who perished in a *horrendous* road accident just recently, and whose young brother Donny . . . *Danny* . . . has braved the elements on a truly filthy Buckie morning to be with us *live* on the *Breakfast Show* phone-in. Give that man a baggy medal! (*Flicks switch.*)

Caller Excuse me, but I still haven't put ma question to Bomba MacAteer yet.

Lachie Oh-oh. Big boo-boo, Lachie son! (*Punches up raspberries.*) Fire away, love.

Caller D'you remember giving ma mum a pendant?

Bomba Givin' hur mum a *what*?

Caller A gold pendant . . . You had it engraved with 'I'll Never Get Over You – All My Loving, Bomba'. I just found it among her stuff . . . D'you remember ma mum?

Bomba (*to Lachie, wrapping mitt round mike*) Get this dighted doll off the line ur I'm walkin', pal!

Lachie (*trying to locate phone-in cut-off*) Yes, sirree, an interesting bitty blether there with regard to a piece of Majestics' memorabilia, and let's stay in that nostalgic mood with a classic piece of sixties soul from . . . bugger.

Caller She died last Friday from cancer.

Bomba Right, that's it . . . (*Dunting Danny awake.*) C'mon, you . . . *move*!

Danny is disorientated, and the pair of them have a hard time removing their headphones and disentangling the leads.

Caller D'you want to know when she had me?

Dennis comes to Bomba and Danny's aid while Lachie tries desperately to cut off the phone-in line. He succeeds only in making it louder.

The first of May, 1965 . . . exactly nine months to the day after the Majestics' concert!

Danny and Bomba are released at last. Dennis fetches Lachie a satisfying whack with his rolled-up Rolling Stone *before he, Bomba and Danny stumble out of the studio.*

Caller Hullo, am I still through to . . .?

Lachie succeeds in cutting phone-in line and punches up the next record.

Lachie The Majestics – 'Love Hurts'.

Lights up on Noreen. 'Love Hurts' carries over as she downs the last handful of pills from the bottle. Sound of bath taps running. Noreen's head slumps onto her chest. She slides to the floor, the empty bottle rolling from her hand.

Blackout.

Lights up on Eddie and Miss Toner waiting at railway station taxi-stand with their luggage.

Miss Toner How come thur wasny a trolley on the train? Where's all the taxis? I'm ravenous. Hope they do a decent breakfast at this joint . . . better'n that last hotel you took us . . . a scabby bitta toast wi' an egg that looked like it was laid by a tortoise. C'mon, hurry up, will you! Oh-oh, don't look now, Mr Clockerty, but guess who was on the same train?

Eddie (*alarmed*) It wasn't *Mrs* Clockerty, was it? I'm supposed to be at the British Trouser Fair in Harrogate.

Miss Toner Don't be daft, it was *hur* – the 'pregnant vocalist' that crashed the Cortina. I've still got the burns on ma legs . . . look.

Eddie Where? (*Turning to look for Glenna.*)

Miss Toner (*pointing out marks on her legs*) There . . . there . . . an' thur's one jist . . . Och, see you! I told you not to turn round, she'll be comin' to talk to us now! (*As Glenna comes over.*) Hi, stranger, what brings *you* to Buckie?

Glenna I've got a wee surprise with me for Vincent.

Miss Toner Aw, yuv had it then? Jist lookin' around for its carrycot . . . What you kickin' us for, Mr Clockerty?

Glenna (*producing lumberjacket from one of numerous bags.*) What d'you think?

Miss Toner Aw, my God . . . (*Having to turn away.*) What d'*you* think, Mr Clockerty, 'cos I'm stumped.

Glenna What'd she say?

Eddie She said it's very . . . (*Taking lumberjacket and holding it up.*) It's certainly very – how do you say? – *chunky.* I could maybe place one or two of these with our flagship store, San Diego Misfits. Is this all hand-done?

Miss Toner Chuck flannellin' – it looks like it's been knitted by a colour-blind Martian furra chimpanzee.

Glenna Gimme that! (*Grabs lumberjacket and stuffs it back in bag.*) Vincent was right . . . I think you are two of the most horrible people I've ever met in my whole life!

Miss Toner

Glenna

She storms off towards the end of the taxi queue with her collection of bags. Several other travellers have joined the queue by now.

Eddie No, wait . . . come back to the front of the queue, er . . .

Miss Toner Glynis.

Eddie . . . *Glynis.*

Glenna If anythin', you're even more horrible than she is . . . and it's *Glenna.*

Eddie looks daggers at Miss Toner.

Eddie You know, Janice, sometimes I think you're just too – what's the word?

Miss Toner Intelligent? Sophisticated? Well-read?

Eddie No . . . gallus. Yes, that's it . . . *gallus.*

Miss Toner I like bein' *gallus*! Look at you, yur jist a jumped-up haberdasher in a camel coat an' a semi-detached villa to go wi' the semi-detached intellect that thinks it's highly amusin' to consort wi' low-lifes like Wee Tommy Cairns who could run rings round you when it comes to organisin' a Silver Jubilee tour an' cookin' the books so it looks like Clockerty Enterprises's gonny be in the black when it's actually Wee Tommy that's laughin' all the way to the banks of Loch Lomond an' a Georgian mansion set in four hunner acres. Taxi!

Lights up on Fud, tucking in to a hearty breakfast. Bomba sits opposite, staring into space, practically catatonic. Vincent is seated by himself, leafing through the Daily Record. *Danny appears for breakfast.*

Suzi (*passing on way to bathroom*) Two three-minute eggs and don't eat all the toast, I'm away for my bath.

Danny Mornin', Vinnie. Wife huvvin' a long lie, yeah?

Vincent She's up the stair washin' a coupla shurts fur us.

Danny (*looking for service*) Where is everybody?

Vincent You want to get that burd of yours to do likewise . . . Nothin' worse'n an off-duty Majestic in manky apparel.

Danny pings service bell.

Fud 'Fraid yur outta luck, Danny Boy. Cook's jist went out wi' hur coat on. Right, Bomba?

Bomba is oblivious as Fud commandeers his Arbroath smokies.

Danny Aw, that's jist dandy, that is . . . I should've took up Wacky Lachie's offer an' hud some hot porridge out the dispensin' machine in thur Green Room. You got any spare toast you could lend us, O'Donnell?

Suzi (*offstage*) *Danny!*

Danny swipes toast from Fud and Bomba's table.

Danny I'm not here, Kettles!

Suzi appears at a gallop and grabs hold of Danny.

Suzi Bathroom – upstairs – quick – hurry!

Danny crams a piece of toast into his mouth as she drags him off at speed.

Danny (*unintelligible*) Naw, it's okay, I've already been furra jobby.

They disappear off.

Suzi (*offstage*) Get a bloody move on, ya dope, it's an *emergency*!

Vincent Pretty obvious who wears the pants in that set-up. If Noreen spoke to me like that I'd lamp hur one.

(*He stares at TV listings.*) Sufferin' God, yur no' gonny believe what's on the TV the night!

Eddie appears with Miss Toner in tow.

Eddie Ah, Vincent . . . how did your phone-in go?

Vincent studiously ignores Eddie, thrusts the newspaper at Miss Toner, stabs a finger at the TV listings.

Vincent Seven forty-five – BBC Scotland, 'Pick of the Day'. Look!

Miss Toner Aw, that's nice.

Vincent 'Nice'? Read it! It says 'Hit single fraud scandal may prove death knell for Scotland's top rock'n'roll combo'!

Eddie What? Let me see that! (*Snatches newspaper.*)

Two Ambulance Men hurry unnoticed across the background with a folded stretcher.

Vincent (*turning to face Eddie*) And, yea, before the cock crowest thrice, one of youse will betray me . . . Corinthians, verse whatever-the-hell-it-is . . . That's all I'm sayin'!

Eddie For heaven's sake, Vincent, stop advertising it at the top of your lungs. D'you want the entire hotel glued to this *exposé* this evening?

Miss Toner Fat chance, it's up against a rerun of *Postman Pat* on BBC2 . . .

A slow burn from Eddie and Vincent.

. . . The one about the missin' postal order . . .

Fud Aw, I love that one . . . kids've got it on videotape –

Another slow burn from Eddie and Vincent.

– in Gaelic. Thur's none of us talks a worda Gaelic . . . subtitles're in Polish which I do huv a smattering of following that holiday visit to the shipyards of Gdansk.

The Ambulance Men make their way back out, still unnoticed, with Noreen comatose on the stretcher.

Fud No' fancy one of yur smokies back, Bomba son?

Miss Toner I'll have it!

She joins Fud and Bomba's table.

Vincent When this TV show goes out, you know that's the Majestics done for, don't you?

Eddie No, Vincent, hold on a second!

He makes to follow Vincent. Danny reappears, wrung out.

Danny Hi, Eddie . . . I can tell from yur stricken features yuv heard the worst.

Eddie I was shown the newspaper.

Danny God, that was quick . . . Was thur a photograph?

Eddie A small one of Vincent in a Beatle suit.

Danny I suppose I better go an' find him . . . Break the news, yeah?

Eddie No need, Danny Boy, it was *him* that told *me*.

Danny What about the guys there?

Eddie The entire hotel knows by now . . . Vincent stood right there and spewed out a whole lot of high-decibel cock and bull from the New Testament . . .

Dennis appears from the street, chomping on a burger.

Danny Aye, funny how it affects some people.

Eddie I'm surprised you didn't hear him. Where were you, upstairs in your room?

Suzi appears, fully dressed. Slips arm into jacket.

Suzi Have you told them yet?

Danny Didny huv to tell them, everybody in the hotel knows, apparently . . . includin' Vinnie.

Dennis (*to Suzi*) D'you pair no' get yours either? (*Sits to finish his burger.*)

Suzi (*swipes offering aside, in a fury*) What is it with you geeks? A woman tries to kill herself and not one of you unfeeling bastards bats a bloody eyelid! What's up with you?

A stunned silence: dropped jaws, wide eyes. Miss Toner, the only one unaffected, carries on eating breakfast.

(*To Danny.*) That's it, I've had it. This's the last stop on my itinerary and the last thing I need in my life. Tomorrow, I'm off. (*She turns on her heel.*)

Danny Naw, hang about, don't go . . . I love you, Kettles!

A lengthy pause. Suzi reappears. Danny looks stunned.

I love you.

Suzi Say that again, McGlone.

Danny (*swallowing hard*) I love you.

Another lengthy silence as they look each other in the eyes. The rest of the breakfast room tactfully 'ignores' the goings-on.

Suzi Nup, even at a third hearing it's still got a distinctly bogus ring to it.

Danny Naw, listen to me, Kettles . . .

Suzi Look, can we discuss this some other time – (*Glancing round the room.*) – in *private*? I'm going to the shops to get some toothpaste.

She disappears off.

Danny Come back here, dammit!

Danny stands his ground while the company 'tactfully' holds its breath, neither they nor Danny certain that Suzi will reappear. High tension. Suzi reappears.

Suzi What is it *now*?

Danny Don't get the stripy stuff, it stings ma gums.

Dennis (*punching the air*) Yo!

Lights up on Vincent and Bomba pacing to and fro outside Emergency Department of Hospital.

Vincent God, I really missed ma vocation . . . I've spent more time in an' outta bloody hospitals in the last coupla weeks than Doctor Kildare . . . Wish somebody hud told us sooner.

Bomba I never knew anythin' about it till the wagon drove through the gates an' Dennis said, 'Wur here.' I goes, 'Wur here where?'

Vincent What kinda drip is she on?

Bomba I don't know what kinda drip she's on, did you no' ask the quack?

Vincent I never got to see hur so I never knew she was on a bloody drip so how could I ask the quack?

Bomba (*stops pacing, listens*) Thought that was our transport.

Vincent You sure you gave him the precise pick-up time when you phoned? Y'know what the bugger's like.

Bomba I never gave him any pick-up time – thought it was you that done the phonin'.

Vincent When would I get the opportunity to phone? I was busy discussin' Noreen's condition wi' hur medical adviser, ya nutter!

Bomba Aye, an' I was likewise discussin' possible grounds fur divorce wi' your wife, ma sister, so how the hell was I supposed to phone anybody?

Vincent disappears into Emergency, only to reappear immediately.

Vincent What d'you mean, 'possible grounds fur divorce'? I'm one of the nicest guys you could ever hope to meet, ya rat-faced bastart!

Lights up on Danny and Suzi. Suzi is sitting on a fish crate with Danny standing at some distance away with his back to her. An awkward silence. Suzi unscrews the top from a toothpaste tube and squeezes stripy toothpaste onto toothbrush.

Danny You know thur's fourteen outlets fur stripy toothpaste in Buckie an' the surroundin' area? I finally struck lucky at the caravan site back there.

Suzi How did you know I wasn't just going to get my usual ice-cool-with-a-hint-of-mint bog-standard-buy-one-get-one-free variety?

Danny 'Cos yur that kinda doll . . . that's what I liked about you at Art School, Kettles. I remember Abernethy bangin' on about the Modern Jazz Quartet an' how uncool it was to dig any other kinda vibe an' you gettin' onty the subway the next mornin' wi' a Mohican hairdo, a ballgown, an' a bloody accordion.

Suzi And here's me thinking you never noticed.

Danny (*turning to face her*) Yur not really goin' back to Glasgow the morra, are you, Suzi?

Suzi What's to stop me?

Danny I could take the laces out ma shoes an' tie you to that fish box, fill it fulla bricks an' chuck you inty the water – that would stop you.

Suzi That would kill me. What are you, a necrophiliac?

Danny Never thought about it . . . Still, if that's the only way I'm ever gonny get you inty bed . . .

Suzi Shuttup. Okay, here's a thought. You've got me into bed, lotsa hanky-panky, lotsa rumpy-pumpy . . . Then what? C'mon, Danny . . . then what?

Danny C'mon, Kettles, cool it, will you? Thur's all them caravanners back there starin' at us.

Suzi Not *us* – *you*. I'm off.

Danny Naw, come back, Suzi, I was jist . . .

Suzi (*as she heads off*) No, don't tell me . . . you were just being a *Majestic*. (*Stops, turns.*) Being a Majestic might've cut the mustard some time back, Danny, but not any more. Especially not with me! Don't you get it?

Danny is left standing alone and perplexed.

Danny (*turning to caravan site*) Don't look at me out yur caravan windas, I don't know what she's talkin' about either!

Lights up on Dennis and Bomba in hotel bar.

Dennis (*to Barman*) Give us a Pepsi, Jim . . . (*To Bomba.*) D'you want another pint?

Bomba Get us a big Coor-vwa-zeeay, I'm feelin' decidedly off colour in the wake of this mornin's upheavals . . . plus that bother wi' Noreen.

Dennis (*to Barman*) Large brandy, pal. (*To Bomba.*) Talkin' about 'decidedly off colour', look what's headin' our way.

Vincent appears wearing the lumberjacket. He has a little difficulty with the sleeve length, but otherwise is attempting to look debonair.

Bomba turns to look as Dennis turns away, shoulders heaving.

Vincent (*to Barman*) Bacardi an' Babycham . . . (*To Bomba and Dennis.*) How we doin', you guys?

Bomba Dig the outfit, Vinnie . . . Didny realise you wur pally wi' Dolly Parton. Is that one of hur cast-offs, yeah?

Vincent It's a present.

Dennis My apologies. (*To Bomba's back.*) You wur mistaken. It isny one of hur cast-offs, it's an actual *present* from Dolly Parton.

Glenna appears.

Vincent Over here, babe.

He waves an arm – the lumberjacket sleeve unfurls. Bomba is forced to turn away. Barman places drink on the bar counter in front of Vincent.

Barman Bacardi and Babycham . . . and what can I get for the young lady?

Vincent *This* is fur the young lady. (*Sticks drink in Glenna's mitt, shoves her away.*) Mines's a *pint*.

Barman One pint of Bacardi and Babycham coming right up.

Vincent A pinta *heavy*, ya . . . (*To Bomba and Dennis's backs.*) What the bloody hell's up wi' youse two?

Miss Toner appears, with Eddie at her heels. She clocks Vincent and does an about-turn. Eddie catches her arm.

Eddie Come along, Janice, we're not here to mock, we're here to comfort. (*Dragging Miss Toner towards the bar.*) Vincent, how plucky of you to show up for a drink . . . Don't you agree, Miss Toner?

Miss Toner faces away from the bar.

Vincent What d'you mean, *plucky*? Listen, don't you start.

Eddie What's everybody having?

Everybody is incapable of speech except for Glenna on the periphery.

Glenna (*calling to Vincent*) Going to get us a packet of them wee Cheesy Wotsits, lover?

Vincent angrily waves her request aside, and his lumberjacket sleeve unfurls to his kneecap. Dennis, Bomba, Miss Toner and the Barman are now rendered virtually legless with barely suppressed mirth.

A Young Blonde Woman appears. She hangs back for a few moments before stepping towards the bar.

Young Blonde Woman Good evening . . . *Daddy*.

Bomba freezes. A chilly silence falls over the merrymakers. Bomba slowly turns round to face the newcomer while Vincent looks on impassively.

The Young Blonde Woman produces a switchblade. Everyone shrinks back in horror. The Young Blonde Woman moves resolutely towards the bar. Everyone takes to their heels. The Young Blonde Woman gives chase.

A high-pitched scream.

Eddie (*offstage*) Somebody get an ambulance . . . quick!

Radio Lachie And we interrupt the teatime news to bring you a World Exclusive . . . (*Botched fanfare.*) There's been a stabbing incident at the Majestics' hotel right here in downtown Buckie . . . more details shortly. In the meantime, here's Big Jazza McGlone with 'Mack the Knife'.

Big Jazza appears on screen doing his version of 'Mack the Knife' from his last resting place – in Hell.

First Act curtain.

Act Two

'Tutti Frutti' on music track. Lights up on Eddie, Fud and Dennis in breakfast room at Buckie hotel.

Dennis (*to Fud*) Ma legs went from under us, I don't mind tellin' you . . . What was thon blade like, Eddie? It was about yon size.

Fud I jist wish somebody hud come an' woke us up, that's twice I've missed everythin'. Furst the phone-in, now this . . . God, talk about bad timin'. Don't suppose thur's much chance it *wasny* his daughter, naw?

Dennis Spittin' double, Francis – same sleekit look about the eyes, right, Eddie?

Eddie The police still have to investigate, but I don't really think there's much dubiety with regard to the young lady knifeman's identity.

Fud I expect wull aw huvty come back fur the court case. What's the bettin' it clashes wi' the Pavilion gig?

Bomba appears, looking like a great weight has been lifted off his shoulders.

Bomba I've' jist left the munchkin upstairs . . . Doctor's put hur under sedation. I asked if he could put hur under six feet of Buckie soil but I don't think he heard us.

Dennis Jist sayin' to Fud here, you could tell right away it was Vincent's big lassie . . .

Bomba Aye . . .

Dennis *and* **Bomba** (*together*) Same sleekit look about the eyes . . .

Bomba . . . right. (*Produces gold pendant.*) 'All My Loving – Bomba'. Wonder how many other chicks he gave one of these to? I've a good mind to get in a cab an' and go up to that hospital an' knife the bastart maself!

Eddie I remember him having a pocket full of those with 'All My Loving – Eddie' on them . . . I presumed they were funeral tokens for Eddie Cochran, but now I'm not too sure . . . Still, that's not the problem, the problem is, do we cancel or . . . ?

Bomba Or what?

Eddie Do we go for a substitution?

Bomba Aw, naw, once was enough, Eddie . . . You wurny there fur the fallout . . . (*To Fud.*) What was thon like?

Eddie Let me put it this way –

Bomba You can put it whatever way you like, the answer's still naw.

Eddie Once the word gets out, this hotel's going to be mobbed . . . People are going to come in their droves just to gawp at the survivors . . .

Bomba Yur not on, Eddie!

Eddie In fact, we can stick that on the posters: 'Live Onstage Tonite – The Three She Couldny Kill Plus Mystery Guest' . . . Get you onto that, Dennis . . . Take Fud there with you, he'll make sure the spelling's right.

Dennis What's that supposed to mean?

Fud (*taking his arm*) C'mon, anythin' to get out this dump, it's givin' us the creeps an' I wasny even there.

He and Dennis make their way out.

Eddie Trust me, Bomba, we've got to grasp the nettle and run with it here. I know what the paying public are like.

Bomba 'No chicks', that was the deal. When I gave inty huvvin' that big eejit's wee bree in the band that was the deal, Eddie . . . '*no chicks*' – remember?

Miss Toner appears. Bomba gives her a dirty look and a wide berth as he goes off.

Miss Toner What's up wi' Laughin' Boy? Somebody pinch his dummy tit?

Eddie He's just a trifle peeved, Janice . . . Any word of Miss Kettles and Danny Boy's whereabouts?

Miss Toner Yeah, thuv eloped.

Eddie *What?*

Miss Toner I was goin' to be thur best man, but I failed the medical. You want to see your face, Mr Clockerty. C'mon, I wouldny worry about it . . . When they catch the 'world exclusive' on the local radio they'll be back here pronto fur an 'eye-witness' account' – it's blarin' out from every shop doorway on the High Street.

She turns on TV set.

Eddie What're you doing, Janice? It won't be on the news until . . . oh my God, I completely forgot . . .

Miss Toner (*opening her box of chocolates*) You excited? Me too. Here. (*Offering Eddie a chocolate.*)

Eddie (*putting his head in his hands*) What've I done to deserve this, Miss Toner?

Miss Toner Go on, it's only a hazelnut cluster, I'll manage the rest.

TV Announcer This is BBC Scotland. It's just coming up to seven forty-five and for those of you with the current issue of the *RadioTimes* open in front of you, it's time to go 'Rockin' Thru the Rye'. (*Pause.*) However, owing to problems beyond our control, we're now showing a repeat of the Hogmanay edition of *The Beechgrove Garden.*

'Beechgrove Garden' signature tune plays.

Miss Toner Aw, naw, I was lookin' forward to you makin' a total arse of yurself, Mr Clockerty.

Eddie Thank you for that ringing endorsement, Janice, but you'll still have the opportunity to have fun at my expense. It's merely a reprieve. Here, you can have your hazelnut cluster back. (*Drops it back in the box.*)

Miss Toner D'you think you could be quiet? I'm just about to watch them repotting their tubers.

Eddie Never mind thur tubers, let's you and I get to the gig and see how The Three She Couldny Kill Plus Mystery Guest are getting on.

He and Miss Toner move through to join the audience at the Deep Sea Ballroom gig.

Lights up on Suzi and Danny onstage, with Fud on bass and Dennis depping for Bomba on drums.

Suzi *and* **Danny** (*together, sing*)
'Love . . . love is strange . . . yeh-eh-eh . . .
Lots of people take it for a game.
Once you've got it you never wanna quit, no-oh-oh . . .
After you've had it you're in an awful fix.
Love is strange . . . love is strange.'

Bomba (*from darkness*) Hey there, Danny Boy . . .

A puzzled Danny looks thisaway and that. Bomba strolls into the light from thataway.

How you gonna call your baby on home when she left you, huh?

Suzi

He ousts Dennis from the drumstool and grabs his sticks. The band immediately picks up.

Danny Well, *Bambi* . . . I guess if I wanted her back real bad I think I'd call her on home somethin' like this . . .

(*Sings, to Suzi.*)

'Baby . . . ma sweet baby . . .
Ma sweet baby . . .
Please come on home . . .'

Fud (*appreciatively*) That oughta do it, Danny Boy.

Suzi (*leaning into mike, to Danny*) Nice try, McGlone, but I'm still going back to Glasgow tomorrow . . . as long as you realise that.

Danny See if I care.

Suzi *and* **Danny** (*together, sing*)
'People don't understand . . . oh-oh-oh . . .'

Lights up on groggy Glenna, the bloodstained lumberjacket draped round her shoulders.

Suzi, Danny *and* **Glenna** (*together, sing*)
'They think love is money in the hand,
Your sweet love is better than a kiss . . .'

Lights up on Vincent on trolley. He is placed next to Noreen, in hospital bed. Both are unconscious.

Suzi, Danny *and* **Glenna** (*together, sing*)
'Yeah-eh-eh . . . the way you love me . . .
Sweet kisses I miss. Love is strange . . .
Love is strange. Love is strange.'

Bomba That's yur certificate.

He hands Suzi a scroll.

Suzi What's this, my O level in 'Musical Appreciation'? (*Unfurls scroll, reads.*) 'For the purposes of a one-off show at the Deep Sea Ballroom in Buckie, we the undersigned have voted you, Susan Kettles, an *honorary man*'?

Danny Congratulations, Suzi.

Applause and 'hear, hears' from Bomba, Fud and Danny. The applause dies away as Suzi rips the scroll into shreds and showers them with confetti before walking off.

Fud That's the trouble wi' dolls . . . canny take a joke, Bomba.

Bomba It wasny a joke, it was a bloody *compliment.* *(Calling after Suzi.)* You should be so lucky, sweetheart!

Lights up on Clockerty Enterprises' Glasgow office. Phone rings. Eddie picks up the receiver.

Eddie (*into phone*) Clockerty Enterprises in association with . . . Oh, it's you, Tommy. Well, since you ask, Tommy son, no, it hasn't. It's been one of the worst weeks of my working life so far. I had to donate a pint of my blood, for God's sake. No, it wasn't for medical research, it was for Vincent . . . Because he lost about four of his own when the big lassie stuck the chib inty him . . .

Miss Toner appears with an armful of newspapers.

Hold on, my Press Officer's just arrived . . . Let me check if we got a mention in the nationals. (*To Miss Toner.*) Well?

Miss Toner Well what?

Eddie Anything in the showbiz columns, I'm asking?

Miss Toner It was Vincent Diver that got stabbed up in Buckie, not Frank Sinatra, Mr Clockerty.

Eddie I'm not paying you double time to work up an act, ya stupid girl, have a look and see . . . You still there, Tommy . . .? Was I telling you I found a pressing plant?

Miss Toner (*leafing through paper*) No mention of the stabbin', but listen to this . . . (*Reads.*) 'If like me you're a fan of *World in Action*, *Crimewatch UK* and *The Tube*, you won't want to miss this Friday's BBC1 feature documentary, *Rockin' Thru the Rye* . . .'

Eddie I'll call you back, Tommy. (*He hangs up.*)

Miss Toner '. . . postponed from last week in order to find a slot for it on the national network. This fascinating glimpse under the flat stone of regional rock'n'roll . . . which may very well result in retroactive criminal charges being brought against at least one named individual who took part in the programme . . .'

Eddie Oh, no.

Miss Toner '. . . is timed to coincide with the live appearance in Glasgow at the climax of their less-than-earth-shattering Silver Jubilee tour by the Majestics, whose lead singer Danny McGlone spills not just a hill but a veritable Ben Nevis of rotten beans to investigative journalist Sheena Fisher during forty minutes of very often grotesque, sometimes painful, but ultimately riveting fly-on-the-wall television.'

The phone rings.

D'you want me to pin this up somewhere?

Eddie You're asking for it, m'lady. (*Picking up phone.*) Clockerty Enterprises in assoc— No, not for pressing trousers, Tommy, for pressing the boys' new long playing record.

Lights up on Vincent in wheelchair, a padded neck brace round his throat.

Vincent (*singing into overhead mike*)
'You come on like a dream,
Peaches an' cream,
Lips like strawberry wine . . .
You're sixteen, you're beautiful, and you're mine . . .'

Bomba, Fud *and* **Danny** (*on headphones, back-up vocals*)
'Waaaah-ah-aaaah . . .'

Piercing feedback howling.

Aaaaaaaaaaayabastart!

They stagger away from the mike, clawing at their headphones, while an incensed Vincent spins himself round in his wheelchair.

Vincent I'll kill him . . . I'll kill that cheapskate bastart! How come wur recordin' in a bloody World War Two bunker after toppin' up the Clockerty Enterprises' coffers wi' the proceeds from wur tour . . . tell us that, eh?

Dennis (*over talkback*) Mebbe canny tell you that, Vinnie, but I can tell you to take five . . . Boy here's jist familiarisin' himself with the board, yeah?

Danny (*as they troop out*) Aw, I don't know . . . I reckon twenty-two hours an' fifty-six minutes to record one an' a half tracks is pretty good goin'. Anybody got an open razor handy?

Lights up on Suzi in her flat, Billie Holiday on the turntable. The front doorbell rings.

Suzi Go away. (*Settling down on sofa with magazines.*) I'm not at home.

Offstage crash as front door is booted in. Suzi sits bolt upright. Suzi's estranged husband Stuart appears.

Stuart Three weeks, Suzi. I telephoned . . . I asked around.

He goes on the prowl looking for clues to imagined infidelity.

Suzi What d'you think you're playing at? You can't just barge in here and . . . (*She is knocked aside.*) Oooow!

Stuart Where've you been for the past three weeks?

Suzi Stay away from me, I'm warning you, Stuart!

She looks around for some object to defend herself with. He grabs her and twists her arm up her back.

Stuart Don't be stupid, Susan . . . then again you always were a stupid cow.

Suzi Yeah, when I married you . . . Ow!

Stuart And you still are married to me, let's not forget.

Suzi If only I could . . . Oooow, you're hurting me!

Stuart Good, because you've done nothing but torture me for the last three weeks! (*Turning the screws.*) Do you have any idea of the mental anguish you've put me through? Answer me! Do you?

Suzi Oh, God . . .

Stuart 'The Cantina,' you said . . . 'We can work things out,' you said.

Suzi You're a liar, I never said any such thing!

Stuart (*overlapping*) I waited for you for two hours . . .

sat there and waited . . . like a fool! While you were off screwing around. Weren't you, ye bitch?

Suzi No, Stuart, don't . . . please!

He hits her hard and sends her sprawling, falls on top of her and pinions her hands.

Stuart That's all you were ever good for, wasn't it, ya bitch?

Leans close to place his mouth on hers. Suzi sinks her teeth into his nose and hangs on.

Aaaaaaaaaaaaaargh!

He breaks free, his hand to his injured nose. Suzi clambers to her feet, groggy. Stuart stares at his bloody palm for a moment, then brings it up and wallops Suzi. She goes down and stays down.

Lights up on Vincent in recording studio. He drives himself manically round and round in his chair while the others sprawl about, exhausted. Vincent stops dead.

Vincent I've got it!

Danny Well, don't give it to me, I don't want to end up in a wheelchair.

Vincent We do a rework of the Righteous Brothers, pull it off the album an' put it out as a twelve-inch single. Get in some burds to lay down some shooby-doos behind the vocal . . . (*To Danny.*) What about that burd of yours? She could be one of the back-up dolls, yeah?

Danny Suzi Kettles we talkin' about?

Vincent If that's hur name, aye . . . Bomba there said she was a passable shontoose.

Danny This doll's the real McCoy. She was a total breath of fresh air on them gigs where you never turned up.

Vincent Never turned up? What the hell're you talkin' about, 'never turned up'?

Danny Didny show . . . went AWOL . . . *never turned up*!

Vincent Listen, ya cheeky bastart, the reasons how come I 'never turned up' wur number one, I was involved in a serious road accident, an' numbers two an' three, I was lyin' on ma back in Intensive Care wi' stab wounds to ma throat an' testicles!

Danny Aw, shut yur face, what kinda lame excuse is that supposed to be?

Bomba Ho! Put a lid on it, you pair, or I am goin' to get extremely *vexed*, right?

Vincent hurtles across the studio to use the payphone.

Fud (*to Danny*) Pssst . . . d'you fancy some Coke?

Danny Aw, God, aye . . . huvny hudda hit since I was last in New York . . . C'mon, let's have it.

Fud (*reaching into hiding place*) Don't let onty Bomba, it's his.

Danny What'm I gettin', a spoon ur a straw?

Fud looks this way and that. Produces Coca-Cola.

Fud Here . . . (*Passing it over.*) Jist sook it out the can.

Danny falls back onto his makeshift bed in dismay.

Vincent (*payphone to his ear*) C'mon, ya dozy bitch, pick up the phone . . .

Lights up on Glenna, sitting on floor of her flat, bloody lumberjacket draped over shoulders, grinding another dog-end into the good carpet which is covered with them. The phone rings and rings unheeded.

Vincent Dozy bitch. (*Slams payphone down.*)

Dennis (*over talkback*) It's the Voice of Doom again, you guys . . . Hate to say it, but wur movin' rapidly inty wur last recordin' tranch an' the boy here's got an appointment to huv his bridgework seen to . . .

Vincent Wur fine! The final track's gonny be *live* an' wur gonny nail it in one take! Ho, what's yur burd's phone number an' *I'll* ask hur.

Danny Ask hur what? Yur no' still on about these shooby-doos, Diver? I'm jist after tellin' you . . . this *burd* as you describe hur, is a *star* . . . She's no' gonny drop everythin' an' come racin' in here to do back-up vocals fur a *has-been*, is she?

Vincent What'd you jist cry me?

Fud Aw, fur God's sake . . .

Vincent I don't think I can believe ma ears . . . D'you hear what he jist cried us? See if I wasny in this wheelchair, I would . . . I would . . .

Fud C'mon, Vinnie, yur only gonny do yurself further mischief. (*To Danny.*) What'd you go an' say that fur?

Danny Aye, right enough . . . I shouldny've called him that. (*Moving towards Vincent.*) You urny a has-been, Diver . . . I take it back. I'm sorry.

Vincent I should bloody well hope you ur sorry!

Danny In order to be a has-been you huv to've been a *somebody* in the furst place, an' you, Vincent, wur a *nothin'* an' a *nobody* to start off with.

Vincent Get me outta this chair . . .

Danny Yuv come full circle, right!

Vincent Get me outta this contraption till I murder this lyin' . . . this . . . (*Clawing at throat dressing, choking on his words.*)

Fud (*coming to his aid*) C'mon, old son, yur only gonny burst yur stitches.

Danny An' I want ma pinta blood back, d'you hear?

Vincent vomits blood.

I didny mean right now, ya eejit, I've nothin' to put it in!

A great roar from Bomba as he is roused from his exhausted slumbers by the racket.

Dennis (*over talkback*) Sorry to bother you, gentlemen, no panic whatsoever, but thur's a small electrical fire broke out up here, so would youse please make yur way to the unmarked emergency exits now, thank you.

Lights up on Glenna's flat. Noreen in her District Nurse's outfit, a box of cakes dangling from a string, stands looking at Glenna.

Noreen Your front door was open.

Glenna I don't need any medical help, so you can close it on the way out.

Noreen I drove past the baker's on my way here from the clinic. I'm Vincent's wife . . . Noreen.

Glenna stirs.

Glenna Oh.

Noreen I wasn't sure whether to get jam doughnuts or rum babas . . . Nice carpet . . .

Glenna (*getting to her feet*) Let me make some coffee . . .

Noreen Is it tufted?

Glenna No, it'll be instant.

Noreen Is the carpet tufted, I'm asking?

Glenna Aw, that? Who cares? It was me that paid for it, by the way . . . just in case you're wondering. Same as I'm paying the rent on this dump – out of my trust fund. Did he tell you I lost it?

Noreen Your trust fund, we talking about?

Glenna The baby.

Noreen (*in shock*) Oh, my God.

Glenna Let me get that coffee.

Lights up on recording studio. Fud replaces payphone receiver.

Fud That's wur management on thur way, you guys.

Bomba Good. Tell the cripple that's me away furra shower.

Vincent The *cripple* jist heard that!

He follows Bomba's departure in his wheelchair.

You wouldny be cryin' us that if I wasny in a bloody wheelchair, ya imbecile!

Bomba disappears off.

(*Calling after him.*) Why don't you furget that shower an' huv a bath so you can do us all a favour an' drown yurself in it, ya two-bit arse-faced *imbecile*!

Fud Why don't we pursue the shooby-doo dolls agenda while wur waitin' an' give whatsername another bell? Glynis? Sorry . . . Glenda. (*Holds out payphone receiver.*)

Vincent *Glenna* – get it right! (*Snatches receiver.*) Believe it or not, that hud occurred to me . . . (*Dialling.*) Show that stuck-up burd of McGlone's a thing ur three . . . 'Never turned up'? Did you hear him!

Fud I also heard him cryin' you a *has-been*, Vinnie.

Vincent Aye, thanks fur remindin' me . . . Where is he anyhow? (*Casting around for Danny.*) See if he isny here fur the last an' final . . . (*Into phone.*) Aw, hullo, is that you, babe? (*A stricken look – claps a hand over mouthpiece.*) I don't believe it, I've went an' dialled the wrong number! (*Into phone.*) Aw . . . er . . . hullo, Noreen, yur back from the laundrette then? I tried phonin' you earlier on but . . . sorry? (*Clamps receiver to chest. To Fud.*) She jist asked me if I want to talk to *Glenna*!

Fud (*frowns*) 'S up wi' that? That *is* who you want to talk to, isn't it?

Vincent bops him with receiver.

Ow!

Lights up on Glenna's flat. Fud's 'Ow!' runs into Glenna's as Noreen gives Glenna a good pasting with the contents of the cake box.

Noreen Here – have the last rum baba, ya wee whore! And another . . . *and* another!

She squashes it into her face.

Where's all his stuff? Upstairs?

Noreen disappears upstairs.

Lights up on Suzi's apartment. Danny is sprawled on the sofa, totally knackered.

Danny I'm only here furra minute, Kettles . . . I've got to sneak back to that underground bomb shelter an' get on wi' hackin' out a long playin' record from a solid lump of acetate the size of Krakatoa before they discover I'm not there.

Suzi (*offstage*) Before I come through, there's something I've got to tell you, Danny.

Danny Yuv no' got any togs on? That's okay, I'll take mines off as well.

Suzi (*offstage*) You know how you asked me a while back if there was anybody . . . a guy – remember?

Danny I think I did quiz you about – (*Yawning.*) – a *chap* . . . Yes?

Suzi (*coming through, a hand up to hide bruised face*) Well, there is . . . *was* . . . *is*. He was here this morning . . . And there's something else you ought to know. He's . . . er . . . he's my husband.

She turns to discover Danny fast asleep on sofa.

Ya big jerk – I'm talking to you!

She leans down into Danny, grabs his lapels.

Look . . . look at me! His name's Stuart Gordon Inverarrity and he's a dentist! You've got to do something! Oh, Danny . . . Danny . . .

Danny (*still groggy*) What? What? (*Shocked awake.*) Aw, my God, look at yur kisser, Kettles . . . Did you say somethin' about a *dentist*?

Suzi is too distressed to respond.

Sufferin' God, that's hellish . . . What was it, a wisdom tooth?

Lights up on Noreen with binbag full of Vincent's clothes. Glenna on floor.

Noreen Get that off! I need it for my bonfire . . . Get it off, I said!

She tears the lumberjacket off Glenna and stuffs it in the binbag.

Lights up on Danny and Suzi.

Danny What in God's name possessed you to marry this dentist?

Suzi He had a lovely smile . . . How should I know? I'd arranged to meet him at the Cantina.

Danny What? How come you had a date wi' this psychopath?

Suzi It wasn't a *date*. I had something to discuss with him!

Danny What '*something*'? You an' him gettin' back together, was that it?

Suzi Yeah, I really missed gettin' ma head punched in. What *d'you* think?

Danny Well, if it wasny that, what was it?

Suzi I'll tell you some other time.

Danny Naw, tell me now . . . I don't like you makin' secret rendezvous behind ma back. What was it?

Suzi Hang off! I'll meet *who*ever I like *when*ever I like, I don't have to get clearance from you or anybody else! And I *didn't* meet him. I arranged to meet him, but I didn't. I went with you to Ardrossan instead, right? Who d'you think you are to say what I can or can't do, anyhow?

Danny Well, that's it, isn't it? That's it! I'm jist the mug that sleeps in the bathtub, takes you out on tour, advises you on dental hygiene, gets kept in the dark about the *dentist* . . . Who am *I* to tell you anythin'? I'll tell you this much – I wish to Christ I was back in that crummy one-room walk-up in the South Bronx right now . . . At least I knew where I was wi' the funny shoe salesman!

Suzi I was trying to explain about Stuart . . . you were asleep!

Danny I've taken ma last cold shower on account of you, Kettles . . . sorry, *Mrs Inverarrity*. (*Heading off.*) You know what you are, don't you?

Suzi No, come back, McGlone . . .

Danny (*disappearing off*) Thur's tons of dolls out there canny wait to sink thur teeth inty this magnificent physique . . .

Suzi No, wait! What about these 'shooby-doos' you mentioned on the phone?

Danny (*offstage*) Tons of dolls, d'you hear?

Blackout.

Lights up on recording studio. Eddie in shirtsleeves.

Eddie (*on talkback mike to Dennis in booth*) Just waiting for the additional personnel to arrive, then it's down to business, Dennis.

Miss Toner appears, with Shooby-Doo Dolls in tow.

Miss Toner That's wur Shooby-Doo Dolls here, Mr Clockerty, what d'you want me to do wi' them?

Eddie Do nothing, Janice . . . Welcome, ladies, to what we all hope will go down in the annals of popular music as an historic event. (*Into talkback mike.*) You there, Dennis? (*Confidentially.*) Listen, I'm not at all sure we can wait for Danny Boy to show up, given that you-know-who has already lost a couple of pints of you-know-what down the you-know-where and there's no cast-iron guarantee that his you-know-whats won't be giving him gyp seeing as how he's been sitting on the buggers for the last . . .

Vincent slowly wheels himself on and nudges the back of Eddie's knees with his wheelchair.

Ah, Vincent.

Vincent Apart from the sixty-four stitches an' the two skin grafts ma 'you-know-whats' ur jist fine, Eddie.

The session guitar player appears – a dirty-looking individual with waist-length hair, woolly hat and Ray-Bans.

Eddie (*to Vincent*) That's excellent news . . .

The session man puts his guitar case down. The name on the case reads T. ABERNETHY. *He takes his guitar out and plugs in.*

Now, where's this dirty-looking individual with the hair down to here and the face like a foosty French cake?

A noodle from Abernethy.

Ah . . . nice timing. Roll the tape, Dennis!

Danny appears at the run and takes up his position behind the keyboard. He counts in Fud, Bomba, the Shooby-Doo Dolls, Abernethy and Vincent, before launching straight into a soulful version of 'You've Lost That Lovin' Feelin'' to rival the original.

The live one-take final track drives on to its climactic finish. A dramatic hush as everyone waits for the verdict.

Eddie Thank you, boys and girls, I'm just waiting for . . . hang on a sec . . .

The tension is unbearable.

I'm told we have a Souvenir Album.

Whoops and cheers from Shooby-Doo Dolls. Collapse from Bomba, Fud and Vincent. Danny sends his music score flying across the studio. Abernethy unplugs his guitar. Dennis starts packing gear away as the Shooby-Doo Dolls get ready to go.

If the Shooby-Doo Dolls would like to speak to our Miss Toner, she'll be happy to reimburse them for their contribution, minus hair and beauty product expenditure. Same goes for our session guitar man. Many thanks.

Miss Toner distributes session-fee envelopes.

Bomba . . . You say that one more time, Diver, an' it's not a wheelchair you'll be in, it'll be a pinewood box! I did not blow the whistle on you, get that inty yur thick skull, will you!

Dennis C'mon, you guys, cool it.

Vincent It was so him . . . (*To Bomba.*) How else would she've found out, well? It was so you, it's written all over yur kisser!

Bomba Two hooses, Vincent . . . I told you no good would come of it, didn't I, Fud?

Fud Leave me out of it. That's all they hud in thur furst-aid box . . . Here.

He hands a toilet roll to Vincent.

Vincent What'm I gonny do now? Where am I goin' to stay?

Dennis Listen, if yur lookin' fur someplace to crash . . .

Vincent (*overlapping, to Bomba*) I wouldny be surprised if it was you that put that big lassie up to stabbin' us in Buckie, ya reptile!

Bomba (*ready to leave*) When you're up the infirmary gettin' yur stitches out, huvva word wi' the shrink!

He disappears off. Vincent propels himself after him.

Vincent It's not *ma* family that's the nutters, pal!

Fud (*taking hold of Vincent's wheelchair, to Dennis*) Load him inty the wagon, yeah?

Dennis Aye, as long as you gag him furst . . .

Vincent (*as Fud shoves him off*) Aye, that's right, beat it, MacAteer! (*Offstage.*) Away home to yur *gonks* an' that plug-ugly mother of theirs!

Dennis (*loudly*) Thur's a choke-lead an' a baseball bat under the driver's seat. Use them, Francis!

Danny has a noodle on keyboards as the Shooby-Doo Dolls and Abernethy quit the studio and Dennis goes about his roadie duties. Miss Toner settles herself on a makeshift bed and draws her coat over herself. Dennis, loaded down with cables etc., puts out the lights one by one until Danny and Miss Toner are left in a pool of light.

Danny I was, er . . . wonderin', Janice . . .?

Miss Toner Wonder no longer, it's quite simple . . . I treat him like durt an' when he dies I get the keys to the shop, right?

Eddie (*offstage*) Are you there, Janice?

Miss Toner God, jist when I was gettin' comfy . . . (*Loudly.*) Comin', Mr Clockerty.

Miss Toner disappears off. Danny noodles into the opening bars of 'Love Hurts'.

Lights up on Glenna as she wanders the darkened streets.

Danny (*sings*)
'Love hurts, love scars . . .
Love wounds and mars . . .
Any heart not tough or strong enough
To take a lotta pain . . . take a lotta pain . . .'

Glenna pauses to apply lipstick with a shaky hand.

'Love is like a cloud, holds a lotta rain . . .
Love hurts . . . mm mm, love hurts . . .
Love hurts.'

Dennis (*wandering across*) Some wee burd that let drop to Vinnie about some of us gettin' 'wined an' dined' on kebabs hus just laid an egg about how some of us might've let slip to Sheena Fisher about the ins an' outs of this *alleged* hit single scam from way back, plus one or two other 'home truths' concernin' wur late PR man wi' an item from his toolbox an' some mouthwash . . . Hope it wasny you, Danny Boy, 'cos when I say 'late' PR man, I don't mean he's died, jist left wur employ. I've got a phone number here for him an' from what I've heard he's looking for work, yeah?

Dennis disappears off.

Glenna wanders off and is swallowed up in the night.

Lights up on Sheena Fisher sipping a cocktail. Danny appears.

Sheena So . . . to what do I owe this pleasure?

Danny drops a room key on the table.

I hope you're not out to seduce me?

Danny God, naw . . . huvny anywhere else to stay. Listen, remember thon time you an' I wur huvvin' that chinwag while the boy was swappin' lenses . . . He really was swappin' lenses, right?

Sheena stays quiet.

Aw, naw, don't tell me . . .

Sheena What's up, Danny? Afraid you've been taken for a fool? Same here! I thought when you invited me for a drink you had more on your mind than whether or not you'd dropped that manager of yours in the shit.

Cocktail Barman takes glass, leaves bill.

I need a cab. (*To Danny.*) You're a disgrace to the family's notoriety! If you had one ounce of regard for your dead brother's reputation you would've had me in the elevator by now and then had me again in the shower before we'd even gotten round to ordering room service. *Goodnight!* (*As she stalks away in high dudgeon.*) Where *are* all the Beasts of Rock in this town?

She disappears off. Danny glances at the bar bill.

Danny *How* much? Good grief.

A huge yawn. He picks up the room key and stumbles off.

Lights up on dentist's waiting room. Young couple and older patient are waiting to be seen. High-pitched whine of dental drill over easy-listening radio music.

Radio DJ The Dorbie Henderson Quartet there with 'Serenade without End' . . . and just before we hand over to Archie Peach and his mid-morning *Easy-on-the-Ear Half Hour*, we've been asked by Strathclyde Police to broadcast an urgent appeal for anyone who may be able to identify the body of a young woman, thought to be in her mid- to late teens, found in the river last night close to the Clyde Street suspension bridge . . .

Danny appears, a little ragged from the night before.

She's believed to have entered the water from the bridge some time between ten p.m. and midnight. If you or someone you know has a friend or family member who may have been in that area of the city around that time, would you please call oh-eight-hundred-double-zero-double-zero-nine . . .

Danny slips a handful of Polo mints into his mouth, crunches them. More 'easy-on-the-ear' muzak from the radio. Danny spits 'broken teeth' into his hand. The young couple look away in disgust while the older patient peruses a magazine.

Danny Jist after bitin' inty an undercooked carry-out *kebab* . . . Look, you can still see the green meat clingin' to that broken bicuspid.

Young Man Know what?

Young Woman Yur toothache's gone? Mine too.

Young Man C'mon.

They beat a hasty retreat.

Danny Young folk, what they like, eh?

Older Patient I don't know who you are, but you're *disgusting.*

He stomps off.

Danny Aye, but when I wake up in the mornin' I'll *still* be disgusting, whereas when you wake up . . . (*Stops, frowns.*)

Stuart appears in a dental smock, a plaster across his nose.

Stuart Mr Malone?

Danny *McGlone.* Mr Inverarrity, I presume?

He approaches Suzi's estranged husband. Stuart looks around at empty chairs.

Stuart You appear to have chased away all my other clients . . . Now, why would a nice big chap like you do such a thing . . . hmm?

Danny Because 'nice big chaps' like me don't like smooth-talkin' weirdos like you that get thur rocks off from beatin' up thur wives . . . Inside!

He grabs Stuart and shoves him back into his surgery.

Stuart Hang on! What the hell d'you think you're . . . (*As they disappear offstage.*) Oooow! No . . . help! Let go of me . . . no . . . not *that* . . . no, please . . .

High-pitched whine of dental drill.

Waaaaaaaaaaaaaaaaaaaaaaaaagh!

Lights up on Vincent, now on crutches and dressed from head to toe in black – shattered, bereft. He looks around the dead Glenna's flat.

Dennis appears with Danny in tow. Danny has a small holly and mistletoe wreath behind his back. Dennis points at Danny's shoes. Danny removes his footwear. Dennis disappears off.

Danny Thur was a fruiter's jist along from the dentist's. I'm afraid that was all they had in the way of . . . you know . . .

Vincent (*accepting wreath*) Naw, naw, it's . . . er . . . (*Staring at it for some time.*) I'm touched.

He teeters on the brink of an emotional precipice.

Danny Hang on . . . (*Pats pockets, locates the right one and withdraws papier-mâché robin.*) Wasny too sure whether to leave it on or . . . (*Straightens its beak.*) Anyhow, there you go.

Vincent reaches out a trembling hand and takes the robin, examines it, not entirely certain what it is.

It's a robin.

Vincent Really?

He places it carefully along with the wreath beside other tributes.

She was very fond of robins . . . (*Picks up small framed photograph.*) That's one hur an' I hud took at Seamill jist after we'd went to see *A Hunner an' One Dalmations.*

Danny (*taking snap, ponders it*) Guy up our street used to huv a paira swimmin' trunks identical to these.

Vincent swings off round the room on his new crutches, picking up a two-thirds-full bottle of whisky en route. The lengthy silence that follows is filled with feelings and emotions they both share.

I was the same when the Big Guy went. It's like thur's a dam.

Vincent Exactly. Right here . . . (*Thumping his chest.*) An' it feels like it's never goin' to burst! I mean, you don't go out yur road to fall head over heels furra doll, it jist happens, right?

Danny You can say that again . . . One minute yur jist an Ordinary Joe, across' fur yur Big Bree's funeral service, an' some palooka drops you off somewhere in yur home town an' you canny recognise where you are 'cos it's changed that much, an' you wander inty this Mexican dive an' yur sittin' there huvvin' yur own nightmare stroll down Memory Lane when this broad you huvny seen since Art School comes up an' yur halfway through the usual ping-pong patter when *bang*! Yur a basket case . . . canny eat, canny sleep . . . all you want to do is hang about with hur fur the rest of yur natural . . . I know precisely what you mean, Vinnie.

Vincent (*snapping out of trance*) What'd you jist say?

Danny What – 'One minute yur jist an Ordinary Joe'?

Vincent Naw . . . you jist called us 'Vinnie'.

Danny So? That's yur name, innit?

Vincent Aye, but that's the furst time yuv ever called us it!

Danny C'mon, it's hardly what you'd describe as the Miracle at Lourdes.

Vincent I know, I know, but d'you no' see, Danny?

Danny *Snap!*

Vincent What?

Danny That's the furst time you've ever used ma furst name without tackin' a derisory 'Boy' onty the end of it. (*Wiping moist eye.*) 'Scuse me while I visit yur cludgie . . . Overflowin' tear ducts . . . bad fur ma image. (*Makes to leave.*)

Vincent (*swiping at own eyes*) What about *ma* bloody image?

Danny What *image*? You huvny *got* an image, Diver.

Vincent The Iron Man of Scottish Rock, pal!

Danny Sorry, say again? I didn't quite . . .

Vincent The Iron Man of Scottish . . . The Iron Man of . . . The Iron Man . . . (*Wiping nose with sleeve.*) The Iron. . . . aw, Christ. (*Crumpling.*) Christ!

Buries his face in his hands. His knees buckle. The crutches go. The dam is finally breached.

Lights up on Eddie's office. Fud is looking at the death notices in a newspaper while Bomba looks thoughtful.

Fud Know what hur second name was?

Bomba (*preoccupied*) Eh?

Fud McFadden. The Munchkin . . . Glenna McFadden. It says here. 'No Flowers'.

Eddie appears.

Eddie So, what's the verdict? Have you run that suggestion of mine up the flagpole?

Fud Aye, an' it never even got to half-mast, Eddie.

Bomba Naw, naw, let's not be too hasty here . . .

Fud What? Thought you an' I wur agreed?

Dennis appears.

Dennis How we doin', you guys? Everythin's settled, yeah?

Eddie I think we might have an overall majority . . . Let's have a show of hands.

His hand and Dennis's go up. They look to Bomba.

Bomba (*to Fud*) Chuck starin' at us.

Eddie Unless, of course, you want to see the band and all its back-up machinery disappear down the stank, which is what's going to happen if we don't *do* something about this travesty on the TV tomorrow night.

Dennis (*to Bomba*) C'mon, I hud the sap sussed furra stool pigeon as soon as I seen him at the cemetery, so what you waxin' sentimental fur? Get the hand up.

Bomba slowly raises his hand.

Eddie Good. (*Picks up phone, dials.*) Help yourself to some of Mrs Clockerty's home-made Trail Mix, Francis. (*Shoves bowl across the desk.*)

Bomba (*to Fud*) Chuck starin' at us, I said!

Eddie (*into phone*) Hullo, Miss Fisher? Eddie Clockerty here.

Dennis takes Fud and Bomba off.

What say you and I rendezvous tomorrow to discuss this on-screen disclaimer concerning the boy McGlone's mental health . . .? I've just received his psychiatric report card from the States. Let me treat you to a cocktail at the Polo Lounge . . . (*A little laugh.*) No, the one on Jamaica Street . . . next door to the Zoo Up A Close.

Lights up on Vincent and Danny. Vincent is sprawled in a chair, his crutches abandoned for the moment. Danny tops up Vincent's coffee mug from a whisky bottle.

Vincent I can still smell thon perfume I bought hur in Lossiemouth. . . . (*Taking deep lungful.*) Hud ourselfs an all-day breakfast at thon wee joint on the seafront yonder . . . Hud a go on the swings, bought a beachball, went in swimmin', hired a coupla bikes . . . She fell off hurs, skint hur knees . . .

Danny (*to himself*) Sufferin' God in Heaven, what next? A blow-by-blow account of thur furst canoodle up the back stalls at the Picture House in Wick?

Vincent What'd you say?

Danny I said I'm tryin' to decide on ma get-up fur the morra night – the chocolate two-piece or the old Bacofoil number. Climax gig . . . What d'you think?

Vincent I'm thinkin' about Glenna.

Danny C'mon, all the thinkin' in the world isny gonny bring hur back . . . Here. (*Tops up coffee mug.*) That's yur last, right?

Vincent raises mug to lips. Stops.

Vincent Y'know somethin', Danny Boy? I don't think I can face it.

Danny Good. (*Takes mug from Vincent.*) D'you want me to flush it down the lavvy? Save you gettin' up, yeah?

Vincent The Pavilion, I'm talkin' about. (*Grabs mug back.*)

Danny What . . . the Iron Man of Scottish Rock? What you givin' us, Diver?

Vincent I'm goin' to be fifty-four years of age on the twenty-ninth of next month, that's what I'm givin' you. I'm shagged out from sittin' hunkered up in a soddin' Transit van fur the last six weeks kiddin' maself on I'm lovin' every minute of it . . . (*Relieves Danny of whisky bottle, helps himself.*) I'm fed up playin' the same old riffs to the same old riff-raff fur the same old amount of washers we used to get when we played the self-same dives in the good old, bad old days of yore . . . An' before you say, why don't you put a tune to that, we huvny hud a hit record since nineteen furget-about-it, an' even that was a fix, so thur's not much likelihood of us huvvin' another one, right?

Danny Couldn't agree more.

Vincent I've hud ma skull splut open . . . ma musical competence queried . . . ma motor burnt out . . . ma good clobber destroyed by an arsonist, includin' a hand-crafted item of gents' knitwear of great sentimental value . . . I'm now lumbered wi' two households to find the rent fur an' no offspring that I know of except furra big quine from Buckie that turns out to be Jack-the-bloody-Ripper in stilettos!

Danny Yeah, that was unfortunate.

Vincent An' to cap it all, I've lost the one person in the entire world I ever cared two cents fur . . . (*Takes cigarette from packet.*) Where's that lighter she gave us?

Danny picks up lighter, examines inscription on it.

Danny I sincerely hope fur your sake this isny true, Vinnie.

Vincent What isny true? (*Sticks cigarette in mouth.*)

Danny (*reading lighter*) 'VD from Glenna'.

Flicks lighter to light cigarette. Can't get it to work.

Vincent (*snatching lighter*) Don't you *Vinnie* me, ya bastart. (*He can't get lighter to work either.*)

Bomba, Fud *and* **Dennis** (*offstage, sing*)
'Dum-dum-dum dummy doo-wah . . . oh oh oh . . .
(*Appearing.*) Shooby doo-wah,
Dum-dum-dum dummy doo-wah,
Only the lonely . . .'

Vincent (*plucking unlit cigarette from his lips, sings*)
'Only the lonely
Know the way I feel tonight,
Only the lonely
Can know this feelin' ain't right . . .' (*Etc.*)

Bomba, Fud, Dennis and Danny provide back-up as Vincent gives voice to his hurt. At the end of the number he is a spent force. They lower him onto a chair.

Dennis Mind his crutch.

Bomba D'you want to tell him, or d'you want me to do it, Francis?

Danny Tell him what? Don't think he's in a fit state fur anybody to tell him anythin' . . . Vincent, we talkin'?

Fud Naw, you, Danny Boy . . . We hud a meetin' at Eddie's office . . . Vincent's name certainly came up . . . God, how do I put this?

Danny Naw, yur awright . . . (*Reaching into pocket.*) A fiver okay, yeah?

Fud You tell him, Bomba.

Danny More'n a fiver? Good grief, what we gettin' him, a set of *gold-plated* crutches an' a session wi' a Harley Street bereavement counsellor?

Dennis Allow me. Yur out, Danny Boy.

Danny Hang on, I think I might huv a . . . *What?*

Dennis (*to Fud and Bomba*) C'mon, you guys, let's hit the road.

Dennis passes Fud and Bomba their footwear, sticks his feet into his boots. They head off.

Fud (*over shoulder, to Danny*) I was outvoted three to one . . . Jist want you to know that.

They disappear off.

Danny Naw hold on, you guys . . . What d'you mean, 'out'? Outta *what*?

Lights up on Eddie and Suzi at the Parthenon Greek taverna.

Eddie (*craning round*) Could Miss Kettles here have a big retsina, Ronnie? Oh, and a large ouzo. *Grazie tanto.*

Suzi What d'you mean, he couldn't face me? The only reason I got out of my sick bed at my brother's house in Dunoon was to get here to see Danny.

Eddie (*scanning menu*) The young woman isn't going to press charges, you'll be pleased to hear.

Suzi What? Which 'young woman', what 'charges'?

Eddie Well, to put it in a nutshell, the whole sorry saga kicked off just after we'd put the Souvenir Album to bed. Miss Toner said he even tried it on with her . . .

Suzi Tried what on? Who're we talking about . . . Danny? You're joking.

Eddie I wish I was, but that's not the real nub of the story . . .

Suzi I'm not sure I want to hear the 'real nub', but carry on.

Eddie Well, apparently . . . (*Looking this way and that.*)

Suzi C'mon, hurry up, get on with it.

Eddie . . . apparently our friend booked himself into a double room at the nearest Holiday Inn and after a poolside assignation with none other than – (*Silently mouthing.*) – Sheena Fisher . . .

Suzi Sheena Fisher?

Eddie *Please* . . . keep your voice down! Miss Fisher and I are in top-level talks at the moment, this is entirely between you, I, and the nearest gatepost.

Suzi Right.

Eddie So . . . after a poolside assignation with you-know-who, at which a great deal of drink was taken . . .

Suzi How much drink?

Eddie I believe the bar bill was astronomical – plus the mini-bar in their room was all but decimated . . . empty miniatures all over the shop. Oh, and the shower curtains had been ripped from their moorings so one can only presume there was a certain amount of . . . how shall we say? *Horseplay.*

Suzi (*covering her ears*) That's it, I've heard enough, where d'you want me to sign?

Eddie (*placing contract on table*) The sound-check doesn't get under way till four.

Suzi (*signing contract*) I'll be outside the stage door at a quarter to.

Eddie This calls for a celebration. Would you care to bring us two Macedonian Fruit Amphoras, Ronaldo?

Lights up on Bomba and Fud at Manhattan Casuals. Bomba is in charge of the buggy while Fud selects items from the rail. Miss Toner gets ready to go home. The twins are very quiet.

Bomba (*leaning over buggy, sniffs*) Huv you been givin' these weans drink, Janice?

Miss Toner What was I supposed to do, pick them up an' suckle them?

Bomba Naw, but you could've . . .

Miss Toner Could've nothin'. Lookin' after that pairra Cabbage Patch Dolls single-handed while you an' him are off livin' it up at the Death Mansion wi' Diver might be your idea of a good time but it certainly isny mines . . . (*To Fud.*) None of that stuff's got a musical discount, the fire sale items are through the back. (*To Bomba.*) What you moanin' about, anyhow? (*Leans into buggy. Loudly.*) Thur *quiet* now, aren't they?

The twins are startled into a racket.

Your turn . . . Bye.

Bomba What d'you mean, *ma* turn? I take them to the park every Sunday!

Fud (*trying on swanky jacket*) Every *other* Sunday.

Bomba Shuttit, you . . . an' get that off, you look stupit in it.

Fud Naw, I think I'll hang onty it . . . (*Admiring himself in mirror.*) Yull notice it doesny huv a big yella streak down the back like some people's.

Bomba I hope that remark wasny meant fur me, pal.

The Transit draws up outside. Door slams.

Fud That'll be yur lift arrived, *Judas* – sorry, Bomba.

Dennis appears. Appreciative whistle.

Dennis Cool jaikit, Francis.

Bomba What the bloody hell kept you? I've got to get these Cabbage Patch . . . these *infants* across to ma mother's!

Lights up on Eddie and Vincent, Vincent still sprawled in his chair. Eddie removes his hat and spreads his arms wide.

Eddie Vincent, Vincent, Vincent, Vincent . . .

Vincent lifts his head slightly, squints.

Vincent Eddie?

Eddie Vincent.

Vincent heaves himself up into a sitting position as Eddie slowly approaches, arms spread wide.

Vincent (*managing to stand upright*) Eddie . . .

Eddie (*as they embrace*) Oh, Vincent . . .

Vincent Oh, Eddie . . .

Eddie You're drunk.

Vincent So am I.

Eddie (*checking watch*) Oh dear.

Vincent Deary, deary me.

Eddie It's twenty minutes to four.

Vincent The Happy Hour, right? Lemme give the burd a shout . . .

Eddie No, no, I won't . . . thanks.

Vincent It's no problem. (*Loudly.*) Ho! Y'there, Glenna?

Eddie (*turning away*) Oh, God . . .

Vincent Get in here an' pour this man a drink, ya dozy bitch! Where ur you . . . ho! *Glenna?*

Lights up on Pavilion sound-check. Suzi onstage at mike as Dennis tos and fros with equiment.

Fud and Bomba stroll across the stage as Suzi has a strum on her guitar.

Fud Yur top string wants cranked up a semitone, sweetheart.

Bomba An' don't start gettin' uppity, yull be usin' the same shavin' water as the rest of the band.

Fud disappears off while Bomba hangs back, smirking.

Suzi (*into mike*) I'd just like to say what an honour it is to be the first genetically unsound person to be invited to join the fabulous Majestics. Oh, and I'm sure you'll join me in being thrilled to know I'll be having these off next week and a little something extra grafted on downstairs. Is there a donor in the house?

Bomba Aye, very funny. Listen, it's nothin' personal . . . I like chicks . . . sorry, *burds*. I even married one or two burds, fur God's sake.

Suzi And I suppose your mother was almost one?

Bomba Don't you drag ma mother inty this!

Dennis Ho. Should you no' be knockin' lumps outta this

drumkit? It is a sound-check, an' the only sound that's been checked so far is the lassie's there.

Bomba Aw, God . . . chicks . . . burds. . . *lassies*. What possessed me? I musta been mad! Christine's gonny do hur nut the morra night! Where ur you, O'Donnell?

Suzi Who's Christine?

Bomba disappears off.

Dennis Bomba's missus. She made him swear on the twins' lifes he woudny huv any more truck wi' chicks, burds, lassies, broads, bints an' what-huv-you once hur an' him got spliced. Thur weddin's next weekend . . . her second, his fourth.

Danny (*offstage*) Ho! Get that guitar off, ya traitor!

Suzi Who's that? Is that you, McGlone? (*Shading her eyes.*) Who're you calling a *traitor*, ya two-timing big midden? Where are you?

Danny (*appearing at her side*) Onstage at the Pavilion furra Majestics' sound-check where *I* should be an' *you* shouldny. Give us that guitar an' get back home to yur *knittin'*.

He makes a grab for Suzi's guitar. She hangs on to it for grim death.

Let go of it!

Suzi Gerroff!

Dennis leaps onto Danny's back, an arm round his throat.

Danny Aaaaargh!

Dennis Let go of it, Danny Boy.

Danny lets go of the guitar. Suzi falls backwards onto the floor.

Suzi If it'd been anybody else but *her* I wouldn't've minded so much! How could you, McGlone?

Danny How could I what? (*To Dennis, still on his back.*) Do you mind?

Dennis drops off.

Suzi Sheena Fisher!

Danny Where? (*Turning to look.*)

Suzi That's right, make a joke of it . . . I hate you!

Eddie strolls across sound-check stage.

Eddie I did stress it could all be just hearsay, Suzi . . . Are you there, Janice?

Suzi What?

Eddie disappears off.

Eddie (*offstage*) Janice?

Danny Aw, I get it. *Nightmare at the Holiday Inn*, right? C'mon, ask yurself, Kettles, would I be gettin' up to somethin' untoward with some doll jist after . . .

Suzi Not 'some doll', McGlone . . . Sheena bloody Fisher, right!

Danny Okay, okay . . . wi' Sheena bloody Fisher jist after you'd had that tankin' from the dentist? By the way, that musta been some bite you gave him, he still hud a big Elastoplast across . . . (*Biting his tongue. To Dennis.*) Er . . . what way did Clockerty go?

Suzi How do you know?

Danny I don't, that's why I'm askin' the roadie. I want to get ma air fare back to New York.

Suzi How do you know about the Elastoplast? Have you and that bastard been hanging out together while I've been in Dunoon?

Danny Get a grip, Kettles, I hudda bitta bother wi' ma overbite an' the nearest dentist to the Holiday Inn jist so happened to be . . . Awright, I looked him up in the phone book an' went to pay him a visit.

Suzi You didn't . . . What'd he say?

Danny Nothin' . . . after I'd bored a big hole in every one of his top teeth he couldny even talk right.

Suzi You didn't!

Danny I did! With his own drill – it was *brilliant*!

Suzi So are you . . . C'mere. C'mere, I said.

Danny, thrilled, moves in close for expected kiss. Suzi slips her arms around his waist, smiles. Fud and Bomba appear as Suzi grips the flesh on either side of Danny's waist and squeezes hard. Fud picks up bass, Bomba the drumsticks.

Danny Ah . . . ah . . . aaaaaaaahyah!

Suzi Don't you dare tell me to get back home to my knitting ever again, Danny McGlone, d'you hear?

Dennis (*to Suzi*) Right, sweetheart, you can skedaddle . . .

Suzi (*taking Danny by the arm*) C'mon, you.

They disappear off.

Dennis (*to Fud and Bomba*) If we're not outta here in the next twenty minutes the top act fur the night's gonny huv a leery . . . Thur huvvin' to put the poodles through thur paces in the Pavilion car park.

Fud and Bomba run through a virtuoso quickie on bass and drums.

Lights up on Policeman and Stuart Inverarrity, whose lower jaw is swaddled in a scarf. The Policeman is flipping through a Rogues' Gallery on screen. Stuart suddenly points to his 'assailant'.

The Policeman brings up Big Jazza's file: 'Deceased'. Stuart is flummoxed as the Policeman shows him out.

Lights up on Suzi and Danny in bed together.

Danny What d'you mean, 'It was okay'? Three minutes is a whole heap better'n a lotta guys could manage after comin' straight off a Silver Jubilee tour . . . an' it was closer to *five* minutes, I can see the alarm clock from this side of the bed. (*Sitting upright.*) It'll not always be a disaster!

Suzi Is that you finished now?

Danny There you go again . . . That's twice yuv asked me that in the last three – correction, *five* – minutes!

Suzi Is that you finished going on about it, I'm asking?

Danny It wasny me that was going on about it, it was you. I thought it was *fantastic.*

Suzi Yeah. . . *unbelievable.*

Danny Don't say it like that, it sounds like yur sayin', 'I canny believe it was that awful.'

Suzi It wasn't awful, it was . . . (*Hesitates.*)

Danny Steady . . . don't say anythin' yur not goin' to repeat to the music press in forty years from now, like 'mind-blowing' and 'beyond'.

Suzi Okay, you want the absolute truth, Danny?

Danny Of course I want the truth. (*Settling back confidently.*) Right, let's have it.

Suzi It was okay . . . cross my heart and hope to die.

Danny Fine . . . as soon as I locate ma underpants, I'm off.

His head disappears under the covers.

Suzi My mind was on other stuff, that was all.

Danny (*still under covers*) Oh yes, that's precisely what a chap wants to hear . . . (*Reappearing.*) Like what?

Suzi Like tomorrow night . . . and beyond.

Danny Aye, *now* yur sayin' it. Listen, Kettles, after the morra night thur wullny be a 'beyond' . . . certainly not for yours truly. I've been *replaced*, remember? Where in God's name ur these bloody underpants?

Suzi Of course you haven't been replaced, don't be ridiculous.

Danny (*mimicking*) 'Don't be ridiculous.' It's okay fur you to say that, you're the *Majestic*, not me!

Suzi 'You're the *Majestic*, not me!' Come off it, Danny Boy, you're the one that described them as a 'buncha neanderthals'.

Danny See? That's exactly what I mean!

Suzi What is?

Danny You just stuck a 'Boy' onty the end of 'Danny', thereby consolidatin' yur credentials. Next thing we know yull be growin' a setta sideburns an' whistlin' at dolls out the wagon.

Suzi Yeah, I can't wait . . . Listen, stupit-appearance, Vincent isn't goin' to make it tomorrow night so . . .

Danny Aw, that's a great consolation, that is. Furst I step inty Big Jazza's size fourteens, now I'm supposed to step inty Diver's boots? Thanks a bunch, Suzi!

Suzi turns away, convulsed.

Danny What you laughin' at'?

Suzi I'm just picturing you clunkin' around the Pavilion stage tomorrow night in your Bacofoil outfit and a set of *diver's boots* . . . (*Laughing out loud.*)

Danny (*waits his chance*) An' how come you didny trust me? *Eh?*

Suzi (*not quite done laughing*) What?

Danny You don't imagine I spent all those delightful evenings confined to the bathroom without makin' a complete inventory of yur medicine cabinet, do you?

Suzi stops laughing, sits up.

I came across some additional pharmaceutical paraphernalia jist before you came to bed . . . (*Producing packaging from pregnancy testing kit.*) Tahraaaaah.

Suzi Gimme that! (*Snatching it from him.*)

Danny Don't worry, Suzi, now that wuv slept together . . .

Suzi Forty winks, McGlone!

Danny . . . now that wuv slept together, I can in all conscience kid maself on it's mines when it arrives.

Suzi stares at him in disbelief.

I know, I know . . . it's morally suspect, not to mention mildly medieval, but every wean that comes inty the world deserves a mammy *and* a daddy in ma book.

Suzi What is that, a psychiatric condition – a 'father' fixation in which *you* are the father, what?

Danny Naw, naw, it's jist that I think it would be nice to . . .

Suzi You're off your head, McGlone, I'm perfectly capable of looking after my own child when it gets here.

Danny Aye, that'll be right. What you gonny do fur dosh? You need dosh to bring up a wean – food, togs, toys, books. What you gonny do, go back to yur old trade? I can see it now – 'Desperate for a Drink and in a Mad Hurry? Then Come Inside and Be Served by One of Our Pregnant Bar Staff.'

Suzi I'm in a band, amn't I?

Danny Ha! Listen, you're only 'in a band' so Eddie Clockerty can huv a go at dilutin' the possible impact of this TV *obituary* the whole country canny wait to goggle at while thur changin' inty thur good duds before catchin' the show at the Pavilion the morra night . . . Look at the face – you didny think he was signin' you up on yur talent an' good looks, did you? Eddie Clockerty wouldny recognise either of those attributes if you shoved Maria Callas inty a pairra jockey shorts an' got hur to sing 'The Campdown Races', Kettles!

Suzi So what? I don't have to depend on the Majestics, there's about fifty paintings under this bed I can sell.

Danny Like this one, you mean?

Reaches under bed. Holds up a small, badly painted canvas.

Suzi Put that back!

Danny Thur no' very good, ur they?

Suzi Get your manky paws off! (*Grabs canvas.*) Who d'you think you are?

Danny With any luck, the future Mr Kettles. What d'you say, Suzi? I've got the perfect honeymoon spot picked out. I've only got to cable the funny shoe salesman an' wuv got the entire dump to ourselves. Bring yur paintin's, I'll be happy to touch them up fur you . . .

Suzi snaps light off.

(*From darkness.*) Naw, please, Suzi . . . Naw, don't . . . Oooooow! That was really sore!

Suzi It was meant to be sore! Get up and make us some coffee.

Danny That'll be the royal 'us', yeah? Yuv only got the one cup, remember.

Suzi (*quietly*) I bought another one.

Danny Sorry, I didn't quite . . .?

Suzi I bought another cup. On you go, get a move on. The coffee jar's on the top shelf next to the crystallised figs.

Danny I still huvny found ma underpants.

Suzi C'mon, hurry up and find them, then. I'm just getting my feet warmed up after that . . . (*Stops herself.*)

Danny Go on, say it . . . that *fiasco*, right? (*Snaps light on.*) If the dentist was any better at it, how come you left him, eh?

Suzi There are other things in life, Danny.

Danny Ah, so he *was* better at it?

Suzi I told you how fantastic it was, what more d'you want? It was *fantastic* – the earth moved, the bed moved, the flowers on the bloody wallpaper moved! Now, get up and make us a cup of coffee, will you?

Danny Okay, okay, I was only wantin' to get at the truth . . . God, yur such a crosspatch when yur riled. Just one other thing, Suzi.

Suzi *Yes?*

Danny See when wuv had wur coffee, d'you fancy . . . you know . . .?

Suzi A crystallised fig? Don't be daft, they'll be foosty, ya big dope.

Blackout.

Lights up on Vincent in the same all-black outfit, but with one of Glenna's scarves knotted round his throat. Still on crutches, he is making his painful way in the direction of the Pavilion for the climactic Majestics gig. Sound of car door slamming shut. Noreen appears.

Noreen Right, that's it. I've been kerb-crawling behind you for the last two miles. Are you going to be sensible and get into that car, Vincent Diver, or do I have to . . .

Vincent Beat it, Noreen. If thur's one thing I canny stomach it's an 'understandin' wife'. I don't want to be understood – never did, never wull, *understand*?

Noreen Loud and clear.

She turns on her heel and starts back towards her car.

Vincent Well, what d'you expect? I've went an' lost the one thing in the world that you could never give us . . . an' before you come back at us wi' one of yur celebrated one-liners, naw, I don't mean a fitted carpet, I mean a *kid* . . . right?

Noreen Right, you listen to me for a change. She didny do herself in because she lost a kid, she done herself in because she *found* one – *you*, Vincent! When're you going to grow up? There never was any 'kid'. It was a figment of her imagination – a fantasy. She even had me swallowing her juvenile day-dreamings for a second . . . Then I remembered your sperm count.

Vincent Remembered ma what?

Noreen More fool me for letting you believe for the past thirty-two years that it was all my fault. I started to believe it myself. I even told Fud's wife it was me that couldn't have any when she was in hospital having that last wee boy of theirs . . . The look she gave me. I wanted to hit her.

Vincent Hold on a minute . . . Jist you hold on a minute! If what you wur sayin' was true, ya lyin' bitch, what about thon big quine up in Buckie? *Eh?* Furgot about *hur*, didn't you!

Noreen Well, whoever she was, she couldn't've been the fruit of your loins. You don't have enough *juice*, mister.

Vincent Don't you 'mister' me, ya lyin' bitch that you ur!

Noreen Check it out, the hospital's on your way to the Pavilion . . . The lowest sperm count since records began.

Vincent's knees buckle.

Think of it this way, Vincent. You may not've made it into 'The Top Hundred Hit Singles of All Time', but your name's there in the medical textbooks under 'Infertility in West of Scotland Working-Class Males, 1953 to 1986', right at the bottom. Trust me, I'm a nurse.

She makes her way back towards her car.

Lights up on Suzi in dressing room. Eddie has his back to her while she changes into stage gear.

Eddie According to a neighbour, he vacated the bereaved apartment around lunchtime. He was last spotted coming out of a licensed grocer's at the far end of Duke Street . . . on all fours. Since then not a sausage. So you see, Suzi, we're sunk unless . . .

Suzi (*now dressed, combing her hair*) I telephone Danny, yeah?

Eddie . . . Would you?

Suzi Of course, I will . . . except I've no idea where he is. I know where his underpants are, but as to their owner's whereabouts, that's anybody's guess.

Miss Toner appears, gives Suzi the once-over.

Miss Toner I've been huntin' all over the place for you, Mr Clockerty. How did yur cocktail meetin' go this morning, did you-know-who get drunk?

Eddie (*drawing her aside*) No, you-know-who did not get drunk, Janice . . . for the simple reason that you-know-who never showed up.

Miss Toner What is it, an epidemic or somethin'? So, what happens now?

Eddie What happens now is that when this pack of lies hits the teatime TV screens one can pretty much say it's curtains for Clockerty Enterprises in association with Carntyne Promotions *and* the Majestics . . .

Miss Toner Don't say that, Mr Clockerty. (*Has another gander at Suzi's outfit.*)

Eddie What d'you reckon to a fresh start with a yashmak-and-harem-pants franchise in a souk in Abu Dhabi under an assumed identity . . . *Jasmine*?

Lights up on Vincent as he stops in front of a TV store. He catches sight of himself from twenty-five years back.

A primal scream starts in his guts, roars up his windpipe, and explodes through his teeth. The crutches clatter to the ground and he falls to his knees, head back and arms outstretched on either side like the fallen Christ.

Offstage slam of car door. Noreen appears.

Noreen Yeah, okay, Vincent, I *was* lying about your sperm count . . . (*Helping him upright.*) C'mon. (*Pause.*) It was only the second lowest.

Noreen and Vincent disappear off, in the direction of the Pavilion.

Pavilion MC (*from blackout*) Ladies and gentlemen . . . the Majestics.

Lights up on Bomba, Fud and Suzi with Shooby-Doo Dolls and the session man, Abernethy, onstage at the Pavilion. Dennis plugs in Danny's keyboard and quits the stage at a running half-crouch.

Suzi (*sings*)
'You know I can be found
Sittin' home all alone . . .
If you can't come around,
At least please telephone.
Don't be cruel to a heart that's true . . .
Baby, if I made you mad,
With somethin' I might've said,
Please forget ma past,
The future looks bright ahead . . .
Don't be cruel to a heart that's true . . .
Don't want no other love . . .
Baby, it's just you I'm thinkin' of . . .'

Danny (*offstage, sings*)
'Don't stop thinkin' of me,
Don't make me feel this way . . .'

(*Walking into light.*)

'C'mon over here an' love me,
You know what I want to say . . .'

VOX

Suzi *and* **Danny** (*together, sing*)
'Don't be cruel to a heart that's true . . .
Why should we be apart?
I really love you, baby, cross ma heart.'

Suzi Where did you get to? I was worried sick!

Danny What for? I only went to buy some underpants. Got an extra pair fur the honeymoon.

(*Sings.*)

'Let's step up to the preacher an' let us say – I do!'

Suzi I do!

Danny Yahoo!

(*Sings.*)

'Then you'll know you have me.'

Suzi (*sings*)
'An' I'll know that I have you!'

Suzi *and* **Danny** (*together, sing*)
'Don't be cruel to a heart that's true . . .
Don't want no other love . . .
Baby, it's just you I'm thinking of . . .'

The number ends. They kiss. Abernethy picks out the wailing intro to 'Love Hurts' on guitar. Danny joins on keyboards.

Danny (*sings*)
'Love hurts . . .'

Vincent (*from back of auditorium, sings brokenly*)
'Love scars . . .'

Danny (*sings*)
'Love wounds . . .'

Vincent (*sings, making his way towards stage*)
'. . . and mars

Any heart not tough or strong enough . . .
To take a lot of pain, take a lot of pain . . .
Love is like a cloud . . . holds a lot of rain . . .'

Danny, Suzi, Shooby-Doo Dolls et al take up the refrain along with Vincent, as he painfully but purposefully staggers to the front of the auditorium, where Dennis is on hand to help the defiant Vincent up onto the stage for what to all intents and purposes appears to be the Majestics' Last Farewell.

Vincent *et al* (*sing*)
'Love hurts . . . mm mm . . .
Love hurts. Love hurts.'

Danny's keyboard segues out of the plaintive and into the joyous: 'Tutti Frutti'.

Danny (*sings*)
'A-wop boppa loo-bop a-wop bam-boom!
Tutti frutti, all rootie . . .
Tutti frutti, all rootie . . .
Tutti frutti, all rootie . . .
Tutti frutti, all rootie . . .'

Vincent takes a bottle of 140-proof Polish vodka from inside his jacket and douses himself with the contents.

Danny (*sings*)
'I gotta gal name of Sue,
She know just what to do . . .
I got a gal name of Sue,
She know just what to do . . .
She rock to the east, she rock to the west,
She's the gal that I love best . . .
Tutti frutti, all rootie . . .
Tutti frutti, all rootie . . .
Tutti frutti, all rootie . . .'

Vincent has wandered across the stage by now, having located his lighter, and is trying to get it to light as he disappears off.

Danny, Suzi *et al* (*sing*)
'A-wop boppa loo-bop a-wop bam BOOM!'

As they hit the last note there is a great flash of flame as Vincent sets himself alight.

Curtain.